SOCIAL LIFE IN AN INDIAN SLUM

SOCIAL LIFE IN AN INDIAN SLUM

Paul D. Wiebe

CAROLINA ACADEMIC PRESS
Durham, North Carolina

Published in the United States by
CAROLINA ACADEMIC PRESS
2206 Chapel Hill Road, Box 8791 Forest Hills Station
Durham, N. C. 27707

ISBN : 0-89089-051-X
Library of Congress Catalog Card No. 75-5480

PRINTED IN INDIA

Preface

My principal research assistants in this investigation were Stephen Michael and Alladi Vagiswari, both natives of Madras, the city in which Chennanagar (the slum studied) is located. Michael, a holder of a Diploma in Social Work from the Madras School of Social Work, both before and during my efforts in Madras worked under the auspices of the Church of South India's programme for social services. Among his other responsibilities, he had the responsibility of co-ordinating selected welfare activities in the slums of the general Chennanagar area. His prior contacts and familiarity with the Chennanagar context facilitated our entrance here. At all times, Michael was able to associate readily and happily with slum people, in general, and the people of Chennanagar, in particular. I found him to be competent and eager in research.

Vagiswari—a Brahmin girl with an M.A. in Social Work from Stella Maris College, Madras, and a Diploma from the Institute of Public Administration, Delhi—proved to be a little less at ease than Michael in the slum context, but equally enthusiastic. Furthermore, with her excellent education, very keen observational capacities, sensitive personality, and the perspectives she was able to provide in relation to her own social background, she proved to be of invaluable research assistance.

To both Michael and Vagiswari, I owe a very special debt and I sincerely acknowledge it.

Many others helped in various ways. Murdock McKenzie of the Church of South India introduced me to Chennanagar and to numerous other slums. With his long experience and devoted interest in slum work and in work with industrial labourers in Madras, he always proved to be an exceptionally insightful resource person. Numerous people in the University of Madras and in state, Corporation, and local offices assisted me, often going out of their way to be helpful.

Professor Murray Wax of the University of Kansas was my mentor during my graduate studies there and he remains my mentor still. Professor Norman Jacobs has long stimulated my interest in sociology and Indian studies. So has Professor Harold Gould, a colleague always ready, in his inimitable way, to listen to ideas and express his own. Professors Milton Singer and William Form read and made helpful comments on an early draft of the final manuscript.

A study such as this comes out of the assistance such friends and colleagues give and I owe and extend a formal word of appreciation to all of them.

Next, I found the Chennanagar people often frustrated but usually resourceful, necessarily frugal and always eager for any assistance they might be able to get but almost always also happy to share what little they had. From them I received and learned very much. In return, I hope at least that I have presented their perspectives fairly.

I myself was born and reared in India of missionary parents, finishing high school there in 1956. I later (1966-68) did my Ph.D. research in rural Andhra Pradesh (under the auspices of the American Institute of Indian Studies, Philadelphia, and the East-West Center, Honolulu), then the research related to this study during the first eight months of 1970 and the summer of 1971 (under the auspices of the Center for International Comparative Studies of the University of Illinois, Champaign-Urbana). For financial support, I am grateful to the agencies that have funded my work in India. For an early, profound appreciation of what India represents, despite its problems — an appreciation that has continued to grow, independently — I am grateful for the attitudes instilled by my parents, John A. and Viola C. Wiebe.

Finally, without my wife, Donna, and my children, Keith and Cathy, fellow happy travellers to and with India, the work represented here would have been far more difficult to complete and very much less rewarding.

PAUL D. WIEBE

Contents

1. *Introduction*   1

2. *The City and its Slums*   17

3. *Chennanagar*   37

4. *Caste, Family, and Community*   58

5. *Economic Organization*   83

6. *Political Relations*   103

7. *Religion*   124

8. *Schooling and Family Planning*   142

9. *Conclusions*   153

   Bibliography   169

   Index   177

One

Introduction

The general objective of this book is to give a comprehensive picture of the ways in which the members of a slum in Madras socially organize their lives and relate themselves to their various environments. Before proceeding, however, some introductory perspectives might be helpful. And these are provided in this chapter. Our objectives here are simply to gain some appreciation of (*i*) the dimensions of poverty and the problems of slums in India, (*ii*) the nature and quality of the materials on slum life that are so far available, and (*iii*) the theoretical questions we might keep in mind as we proceed. Chapter One will conclude with a more detailed indication of this study's objectives and methodologies.

POVERTY AND SLUMS IN INDIA

The problems of poverty and slums in India are immense. In their excellent study, "Poverty in India,"[1] V.M. Dandekar and N. Rath estimate that 40 per cent of the rural population and 50 per cent of the urban population live below the poverty line, that is, with incomes insufficient even to support diets adequate with respect to calories. They show also that though a superficial examination of survey estimates might indicate that in recent years inequalities in the distribution of consumer expenditures have narrowed down, a more thorough examination of the same figures shows that such a narrowing down, in fact, has not occurred. This makes it possible for the writers to conclude, as they do, that if trends similar to those now occurring continue, the gaps between the rich and the poor in India will widen "intolerably."[2] Dandekar and Rath comment that even now, however, "people not familiar with the 40 per cent poorest rural population and the 50 per cent poorest urban population have wondered how men at all subsist at these levels."[3]

"*Garibi Hatao*" (eliminate poverty) was a campaign slogan used by Indira Gandhi in her impressive electoral sweep in 1971. Certainly it struck a respondent cord among her electors. Yet, no matter how impressive have been the accomplishments of many in the encourage-ment of economic change and betterment in India, the very stark outlines of poverty, as these may be described, remain.

. Meanwhile, and relatedly, the problems of slums in India are also severe. Marked by sub-standard incomes, at best relatively low rates of literacy, bad housing, insufficient medical care, inadequate sanitation, often extremely poor access to public utilities and mal-nutrition,[4] the populations of India's slums often live in appalling physical situations. The problems of slums are not India's alone, of course. Nor are they necessarily worse here than in many other parts of the world—a fact that rightly allows P. Ramachandran to draw some "consolation."[5] Nevertheless, these problems remain as do the processes involved in their development and persistence.

AVAILABLE LITERATURE ON INDIA'S SLUMS

Given the reality of the problems of poverty and slums in India, what understandings of the social life in India's urban slums are there now?

In answer, the best of these must be based on studies conducted (*i*) in relation to Indian Census enumerations—for example, the very good *Slums of Madras City* by P. K. Nambiar[6] (written in relation to the 1961 Census) and the analysis of slum areas of Ahmedabad by R. K. Trivedi[7] (written in relation to the 1961 Census); or (*ii*) in relation to general, socio-economic surveys—for example, the studies conducted in Bombay under the auspices of the Bombay Municipal Corporation,[8] and by S. N. Sen[9] and D. R. Gadgil[10] respective-ly, in Calcutta and Poona. Such studies tell us much about the physical, demographic, health, and crowding conditions and distri-bution of resident peoples according to variables such as place of origin, length of residence, and religious preference. And, obviously, nothing is wrong with such studies and more would be useful. Planners, social workers, administrators, economists, police agencies, "clearance" and "improvement" experts and so on need the kinds of understandings and summary capacities such analyses enable. Urban planning in India (like "rural development" planning) is an important priority at the national, state, and many local levels.

The understandings of slum life possible through such studies, however, are not enough for they tell us "tantalizingly little" (to use a phrase used by F. Bailey[11] to describe other, similar studies) about the substance of slum life, about the ways in which local people relate themselves to each other and to the elements of their environment.

But, in addition to such analyses, almost the only kinds of analyses so far available can only be labelled as thoroughly biased, negatively.[12] A. R. Desai and S. Devadas Pillai, for example, in the general introduction to the book they edit, *Slums and Urbanization*, claim that "all of (the included writers) point to one basic fact: the slum is basically an area of darkness, despair and poverty."[13] Importantly, the contributors to *Slums and Urbanization* present insights enough to enable an easy contradiction of such a generalization and, as they proceed, so do the writers themselves. Nevertheless, the statement given adequately summarizes the formal position taken by the book's editors.

Again, for example, G. R. Madan says the following of the relations between, in his words, "poverty and disorganization:" the poor "...have such a low income that it is difficult for them to manage the affairs of the family...such people become discouraged and cannot perform their functions properly."[14] Under conditions of poverty, Madan continues, "we cannot have healthy individuals, educated children, socialized men and women interested in the progressive development of our social organization."

Again, in the *Encyclopaedia of Social Work in India*, P. R. Nayak claims the "depressed areas" of a city suffer from a low level of community feeling and the "ordinary men" living in these areas, suffering as they are "from a variety of handicaps," have to be helped "to come into their own" and "to become effective citizens."[15]

Finally, for example, S. K. Gupta warns that the social effects of slum living may include "family disintegration, the debasing of marriage and the deterioration of youth through parental neglect."[16] About the possible psychological effects, he agrees with a writer who called a slum a "squalid festering morass of lost hope, debased standards, and despair" adding, broadly, that such a context "generates a morbid mentality and blunts community consciousness and aesthetic values."[17]

Now, no one would doubt that the poor of India's slums are disadvantaged in various ways. Certainly, many of them know difficulties in providing food, medical care, education, and other opportunities for themselves and their children. Then too, evaluations like those by Madan, Nayak, and Gupta no doubt are borne out of concern for the welfare of the poor. But such evaluations, also, strike of the arrogance of knowing about what the poor need, want, and suffer from without the poor themselves having had the chance to participate in the development of the definitions. None of the evaluations just referred to are based on adequate empirical investigations, and all of them "measure" the poor using standards that at least in ways are inappropriate.

Furthermore, such understandings tend to raise more questions than they answer. For example, of Madan we find ourselves compelled to ask: What is "discouragement" for these people? How is it expressed? What functions cannot these people perform properly? Who are "socialized" men and women? And what are "healthy individuals?" Similarly, of Nayak and Gupta we must ask: Is there really so little community organization in "depressed areas?" Cannot leadership emerge of itself in the slum? Is hope indeed lost here? Are local standards of life, in fact, debased? And, even if so, according to whose standards?

Simply, in concluding this section, more sociological understandings of slum life in India must be developed. A number of scholars have already noted this.[18] Our own review of the relevant literature further makes this obvious.

SOME THEORETICAL CONSIDERATIONS

In addition to the basic fact of a need for further understandings, what other kinds of supports might we find to substantiate the meaningfulness of this study of an urban slum? First, as we shall see, it has by now been shown that the view "from the bottom," in any society, is important. Second, current understandings of the definition of "poverty" demand that we gain the understandings possible in such an endeavor. And third, the possible conclusions to a study such as that proposed here tie into a major set of theoretical questions now being asked.

Importance of the View "From the Bottom"

Many scholarly and political analyses of slum life in many parts of the world (including India, as we have just seen) have presumed defects in the mentalities of slum dwellers, explaining the social conditions of these people in terms of their "deficiencies" and "disorganization." Along such lines, slums have often been pictured as cancerous growths or plagues threatening to eat away at their city environments. In fact, slums often do threaten property values, community health standards and so on, and they sometimes do seem to spread in relatively uncontrollable ways.

But more and more it is being recognized that descriptions of the kind just identified are grossly inadequate. The reason here, at least in good measure, is that more and more attention has come to be given to the contexts and consequences of slum living in terms of how these appear from the vantage point of those who themselves are directly involved. Thus, for example, we find that the lower class, Negro street-corner man in Washington D.C., though he generally shares the standards of the wider American society, participates differentially. The differential participation, in turn, is not because of his personal or social "deficiencies" but because of the social, educational, economic, and political disadvantages he knows. Says Elliott Liebow:

...(the street-corner man) does not appear as a carrier of an independent cultural tradition. His behaviour appears not so much as a way of realizing the distinctive goals and values of his own subculture, or of conforming to its models, but rather as his way of trying to achieve many of the goals and values of the larger society, of failing to do this, and of concealing his failure from others and from himself as best he can.[19]

Similarly, other scholars—for example, Herbert Gans,[20] Gerald Suttles,[21] and Charles Valentine[22]—in relation to their own analyses and theoretical formulations, encourage us to view the structures and processes of slum life considering the ways in which slum peoples relate to each other and are linked into their broader social and cultural contexts. Like Liebow, they show us that formulations about slum life that do not take into account the perspectives of slum peoples are likely to be widely misleading.

In introducing her account of what is going on in an urban

neighborhood (La Laja) of a rapidly growing, planned city in the interior of Venezuela, Lisa Peattie supposes that "what is happening in La Laja is neither unique nor isolated" and that, in "trying to understand what is to be seen in terms of the connections which seem to appear between La Laja's life processes and elements of the surrounding environment, some understanding of the surrounding environment, as a new city, as Venezuela, or as one of the typically developing countries" can be achieved.[23] She admits there is something of the ridiculous in this procedure, lightly suggesting it is something like the attempt to understand a dinner party while sitting under the table. Nevertheless, she proceeds. And as she does she allows her reader an intimate understanding of the ways in which environmental processes look "from the bottom."

To look at social life in a Madras slum is to look at social life in Madras at the "bottom." And this, of course, necessitates a considerable caution. The history of Tamilnadu dates back to the centuries long before Christ. Tamil is one of the world's oldest languages and the distinctive dances and music, arts and festivals of Tamilnadu speak for the rich heritage of this general region. Within its region, in turn, Madras blends the modern and industrial with the remnants of colonial times and the strongly persisting features of cultural and social forms that began to emerge in antiquity[24] and still serve to organize socially the Tamils and link them into the wider streams of Indian civilization. A cosmopolitan city, Madras contains people from all of the major language areas and religious groupings of India, and people from many other parts of the world. Though it contains many poor people and many slums, it also contains many extremely pleasant neighbourhoods. Certainly it is true that whatever perspectives of the local context our materials from a Madras slum might provide, we must also view these within proper, more general perspectives.

But understanding this, the view "from the bottom" is very important. First, to repeat, relatively little is thus far known, sociologically, about how the urban poor in India actually live. Second, a perspective such as that possible should help us gain some further understanding of the surrounding Indian environments even as the Peattie, Gans, and Suttles studies enable some understanding of the environments encompassing La Laja, certain "urban villagers," and certain Chicago slums, respectively. And this should help in the development of further theoretical and comparative understandings of social life.

Finally, to the extent that urban planning, slum clearance, and slum improvement schemes are becoming increasingly widely applied in Madras and India, further understandings are necessary of the ways in which the poor—those most often most affected by such schemes—understand these processes and the ways in which these people can be viewed as being able to recreate their own living situations. Even if in many parts of the world, and in India, such understandings do not yet have enough influence over the kinds of practical decisions that effect the poor, it appears likely that their influence will continue to grow. For one thing, paternalistic approaches to slum clearance and slum improvement—where things are done "to" rather than "with" slum dwellers—are proving to be excessively expensive. And they are, for they do not use efficiently the resources and resourcefulness of the people, characteristics identified in various parts of the world by those who have taken the time to learn of them. For another, paternalistic approaches often have been found relatively unsuccessful, in practical terms, when considered along with the responses of those for whom the "improvements" are made.[25]

Understandings of Poverty

"Poverty" and "subsistence" are relative concepts. To use Peter Townsend's words, "they can only be defined in relation to the material and emotional resources available at a particular time to the members either of a particular society or different societies."[26] Or, as J. K. Galbraith puts it: "People are poverty stricken when their income, even if adequate for survival, falls markedly behind that of the community."[27] To divorce definitions of poverty, then, from understandings of the processes of society and the effects these processes have for the psychological well-being of persons within the society and on the capacities of the "poverty stricken" to relate themselves out of their context is to miss the "flesh and blood" of poverty [28]

This is not to say figures outlining nutritional intakes among the poor, income equivalents in terms of national currencies, caloric intakes necessary in specific geographical settings, etc., are unimportant. No knowledgeable person could realistically adopt such a stance. It is to say, on the other hand, that alone such information merely defines the "skeletons" of poverty and that additionally needed are materials pertaining to the ways in which the poor actually command or have access to a society's social, cultural, economic, educational, political, and other resources. The fact that many of India's urban poor actually "make do," is clear, given their numbers and numerical persistence. But not clear, so far—considering again the inadequacies of the literature pertaining to these poor—are understandings of the ways in which they actually do so.

The social and cultural networks of "traditional" India linked together very many disparate groups. The *jajmani* system—a system labelled by the scholarly and very sympathetic student of Indian life, W. H. Wiser, a "most marvelous economic system"[29] —for example, tied into an intricately working system the many occupational groups of a village, in turn also tying a village into its region. So did "traditional" patterns of caste organization,[30] "traditional" orientations to pilgrimages and village festivals,[31] "traditional" political networks,[32] "traditional" patterns of religious observance and belief,[33] "traditional" patterns of law[34] and so on. In short, such systems linked together rich and poor groups, prestigious and lowly groups, powerful and weak groups, into functionally and structurally interdependent networks. These were localized and regionally variant, to be sure. Yet they were also similar enough, in many ways, in many parts of the subcontinent, to blend the diversity evident in the background pages of Indian history into the kinds of unique patterns that characterized the social life of "traditional" Indian civilization. Such things we know. By now we also know, clearly, that "tradition" and "modernity" cannot be considered disjointed within the context of Indian civilization.[35]

And thus again we can tackle, theoretically at least, statements that encourage us to picture slums in the Indian context as cancerous growths and little more. Given the substantive understanding that Indian civilization has given its people many resources and that Indian civilization is marked by very distinctive "unities and continuities"[36] our suspicion has to be that at least some of these remain in service at slum levels. If so, how do they operate? If not, on the other hand—and it is possible that certain older resource patterns do not now persist, given the increasing rates of industrialization, urbanization, and "modernization" that India today knows—what new kinds of resources and access to resources have these people developed? Current definitions of the adequate understanding of poverty demand that we ask such questions.

The "Culture of Poverty" Issue

A topic related to both of the above issues concerns the question of whether or not a "culture of poverty" can be found among the poor. With reference to the just completed discussion, particularly, the question is: Do the poor of a society develop distinctive social patterns and values when considered in relation to the more advantaged? The Liebow, Gans, Suttles, and Valentine understandings imply that they do not. Meanwhile, the Desai and Pillai, Madan, Nayak, and Gupta understandings—even though they are not adequately based in research and though they would hardly be considered important contributions to the "culture of poverty" literature—would imply at least that the Indian urban poor are disjointed from the rest of society, with identifiable characteristics of their own.

Oscar Lewis is the scholar best known for his analyses of the "culture of poverty." And we shall sketch here the outlines he defines. Accordingly, the preconditions of the "culture of poverty" are the following:

> The setting is a cash economy, with wage labour and production for profit and a persistently high rate of unemployment and under-employment, at low wages, for unskilled labour. The society (in which such a culture occurs) fails to provide social, political and economic organization, on either a voluntary basis or by government imposition, for the low-income population. There is a bilateral kinship system centred on the nuclear progenitive family, as distinguished from the unilateral extended kinship system of lineage and clan. The dominant class asserts a set of values that prizes thrift and the accumulation of wealth and property, stresses the possibility of general mobility and explains low economic status as the result of individual personal inadequacy and inferiority.[37]

Where such societal conditions occur, Lewis describes the possible consequent development of a style of life among some of that society's poor—a style that when developed tends to perpetuate itself—as the "culture of poverty."

In his studies, Lewis has identified some seventy traits that characterize the "culture of poverty." The principal ones, however, he describes in four general dimensions:[38] the relationship between the sub-culture and the larger society; the nature of the slum community;

the nature of the family; and the attitudes, values, and character structure of the individual. Regarding the first of these, the disengagement of the poor with respect to the major institutions of the society is seen to be a crucial element in the "culture of poverty." It results in the negative evaluation of the society's major institutions and the development of alternative institutions. In reference to the second, though Lewis allows that a sense of community and a genuine *espirit de corps* might exist in a slum neighborhood and that other kinds of relatively temporary groupings often do exist, he contends that such a community generally "has a minimum of organization beyond the nuclear and extended family," a "marginal and anomalous" pattern of organization in an otherwise organized society.[39]

With reference to the nature of the family, Lewis says that here childhood is not a specially prolonged and protected stage of the life cycle, initiation into sex comes early, the family tends to be mother-centred, there is little privacy, and the female head of the household is given to authoritarian rule. In reference to the attributes of the individual, Lewis says the individual, under such conditions, "...has a strong feeling of fatalism, helplessness, dependence and inferiority."[40]

Lewis' conceptualizations of the "culture of poverty," its underpinnings and consequences certainly are not treated comprehensively in this brief outline. Furthermore, the related arguments, supportive and critical, have been many and heated and sometimes productive of new understandings of poverty.[41] But enough has already been said to enable us a general understanding of the construct's major outlines, as these will concern us here.

Broadly, our research question simply becomes: do the people in India's slums—and, more particularly, in the slum studied here—live in a "culture of poverty?" In his studies, Lewis himself found no such culture in India. But none of these were conducted in places like Madras, Calcutta, or Bombay where, according to his own specifications, this culture in India could most likely be expected. Furthermore, studies such as those cited for Desai and Pillai, and others, lead us to suspect that such a culture in fact might exist in such settings.

In short, the theoretical question of whether or not a "culture of poverty" exists in the urban Indian slum context remains open. And, like the other questions already raised, its answer is important for both practical and theoretical reasons.

OBJECTIVES AND METHODS

Chennanagar[42]—the slum investigated here—was selected for investigation for a number of reasons. First, situated as it is in a developing area of Madras, it promised to be a suitable context in which to examine comparatively, newly emerging and older patterns of social life. Second, in that the Chennanagar people in a preliminary investigation were found to be of extremely varied occupational and social backgrounds, this slum promised to be more suitable for an understanding of some of the diversity represented in the social life of Madras than would other slums inhabited primarily by persons of only relatively few occupational and social backgrounds. Third, it seemed upon preliminary investigation that Chennanagar would not soon be eliminated in relation to major improvement and development schemes. Thus, this slum promised to provide a context in relation to which such considerations would not overwhelm more natural social processes and a context in relation to which later comparative examinations might also be made. Fourth, it seemed that Chennanagar was in the process of becoming a relatively permanent and livable residential area, one where the people were in the process of making a way for themselves, not one that appeared either comparatively "hopeless" or especially blessed by particular outside assistance programmes. Finally—but certainly not least—the Chennanagar people showed an immediate interest in us and our interests in them, and one of my assistants, and friends of ours, already had very good associations here.

Substantively, no specific hypotheses guided our research activities. Rather, our purposes were simply to gain as comprehensive a look as possible at the processes of social life in and "out of" Chennanagar, viewing these from the perspectives of the Chennanagar people.

However, our purposes certainly also fitted into an appreciation for the kinds of questions raised in the last general section of this chapter. That is, they had to do with (*i*) an understanding of the importance of gaining a view "from the bottom" in Indian urban contexts; (*ii*) an understanding of the importance of coming to view slum living in India not only from the vantage point of the outsider but also from the vantage point of slum people themselves; and (*iii*) with a background understanding of the kinds of questions we might ask of the Chennanagar people in seeking to determine whether or not they live in a "culture of poverty." And it is to these kinds of questions that we shall refer in describing our Chennanagar materials and in finally summarizing and analyzing them.

In precaution, Chennanagar is no more or less an "average" slum than at least most of the other slums in Madras. To use Charles Stokes' classification scheme,[43] as we shall see, Chennanagar probably would have to be classified as a slum with more "hope" than "despair" and perhaps it resembles a little more closely an "escalator" than a "non-escalator" type of slum. To the extent that other Madras slums are more characterized by "despair" and "non-escalation," or other combinations or degrees of the two involved polarities —if indeed these can be meaningfully used here at all—our understandings of Chennanagar would have to be adjusted if they were to be used in other places. Many varieties of slums can be found in Madras.

Nevertheless, of course, we shall proceed.

The research for this study was carried out during the first eight months of 1970 and during the summer of 1971. None of us as researchers ever took up residence in Chennanagar. But on an average we spent about four days a week in Chennnagar during the research period. We also visited Chennanagar at odd times—for example, sometimes very early in the morning and sometimes very late at night.

Methodologically, our principal attempts were (i) to observe, (ii) to participate in certain aspects of local life, and (iii) to talk with the people here and in related slums in as many different situations, and as individuals or in groups, as often as possible. With reference to the first attempt, we had open access to all parts of the *nagar* (literally, a city or a part of a city). With reference to the second, in course of time we came to participate in a variety of ceremonies, public occasions, political discussions, and so forth. With reference to the third, in general we talked to as many people as could spare the time.

To integrate understandings thus developed, however, we also conducted sixty-two relatively structured but open-ended interviews with people of many different positions in the community.

We also conducted a careful, census-type survey of all the households in Chennanagar, studied records and reports where these were available and contacted all of the "outsiders" with special responsibilities towards the Chennanagar people. Finally, as we come to find some people particularly good and helpful as "informants," we contacted these people especially often. In fact, we came to consider some of these as very important research assistants.[44]

[1] V.M. Dandekar and N. Rath, "Poverty in India," in *Economic and Political Weekly*, VI, 2 January 1971.

[2] *Ibid.*, p. 25.

[3] *Ibid.*, p. 27.

[4] A.R. Desai and S.D. Pillai (eds.), *Slums and Urbanization*, Popular Prakashan, Bombay, 1970.

[5] P. Ramachandran, "The Slum: A Note on Facts and Solutions," in *ibid.*, p. 167.

[6] P.K. Nambiar, "Slums of Madras City," in *Census of India*, 1961, vol. 9 (Madras), Part 11-C, 1961.

[7] R.K. Trivedi, "Special Report on Ahmedabad City," in *Census of India*, 1961, vol. 5 (Gujarat), Part 10A, 1961.

[8] Bombay Municipal Corporation, "Slums of Bombay," in Desai and Pillai, *op. cit.*

[9] S.N. Sen, "Excerpts from the City of Calcutta: A Socio-Economic Survey (1954-55 to 1957-58)," in Desai and Pillai, *op. cit.*

[10] D.R. Gadgil, "Housing and Slums of Poona," in *Economic and Political Weekly*, XI, 14 April 1959.

[11] F.G. Bailey, "Structure and Change in Indian Society: A Review Article," in *Pacific Affairs*, XLII (Winter), 1969, p. 495.

[12] A.R. Desai and S.D. Pillai have apparently now completed an excellent study of a slum in Bombay (forthcoming with Popular Prakashan Publishers, Bombay), but I have not yet had the chance to see this work. Another exception to the text statement would have to be the work by Gertrude Woodruff on Adi-Dravidas in Bangalore (mimeographed).

[13] Desai and Pillai, *op. cit.*, p. 163.

[14] G.R. Madan, *India's Social Problems: Social Disorganization*, Allied Publishers, Bombay, 1969.

[15] P.R. Nayak, "Community Development: Urban," in *Encyclopaedia of Social Work in India*, vol. 1, 1968, p. 132. This is a Government of India publication issued on behalf of the Planning Commission.

[16] S.K. Gupta, "Slums," in *ibid.*, p. 210.

[17] *Ibid.*

[18] See Dandekar and Rath, *op. cit.*, p. 33; Aprodicio A. Laquian, "Slums and Squatters in South and Southeast Asia," in Leo Jacobsen and Ved Prakash (eds.), *Urbanization and National Development*, Sage Publications, Beverly Hills, 1971, p. 200; and more generally, Charles A. Valentine, *Culture and Poverty*, University of Chicago Press, Chicago, 1968.

[19] Elliott Liebow, *Talley's Corner: A Study of Negro Streetcorner Men*, Little Brown and Company, Boston, 1967, p. 222.

[20] Herbert J. Gans, *The Urban Villagers*, Free Press of Glencoe, New York, 1962.

[21] Gerald Suttles, *The Social Order of the Slum*, University of Chicago Press, Chicago, 1968.

[22] Charles Valentine, *op. cit.*

[23] Lisa R. Peattie, *The View From the Barrio*, University of Michigan Press, Ann Arbor, 1968, p. 1.

[24] Milton Singer, "The Indian Joint Family in Modern Industry," in Milton Singer and Bernard S. Cohn (eds.), *Structure and Change in Indian Society*, Aldine Publishing Company, Chicago, 1968.

[25] "Urbanization: Development Policies and Planning," in *International Social Development Review*, No. 1, United Nations, 1968.

[26] Peter Townsend, "The Meaning of Poverty," in *British Journal of Sociology*, 13, September 1962, p. 210.

[27] J.K. Galbraith, *The Affluent Society*, Hamish Hamilton, London, 1958, p. 252.

[28] Peter Townsend, *op. cit.* p. 220.

[29] W.H. Wiser, "The Economics of Poverty," in *The Allahabad Farmer*, X, November 1936.

[30] Milton Singer, "The Social Organization of Indian Civilization," in *Diogenes*, 45, April 1964.

[31] J. Gumperz, "Religion and Communication in Village North India," in E.B. Harper (ed.) *Religion in South Asia*, University of Washington Press, Seattle, 1964; and M. Marriott, "The Feast of Love," in Milton Singer (ed.), *Krishna Myths, Rites, and Attitudes*, East-West Center Press, Honolulu, 1966.

[32] W.C. Smith, "The Ulama in Indian Politics," in C.H. Phillips (ed.), *Politics and Society in India*, George Allen and Unwin Ltd., London, 1963; and Ravinder Kumar, "Rural Life in Western India on the Eve of the British Conquest," in *Indian Economic and Social History*, 2, July 1965.

[33] M.N. Srinivas, *Religion and Society among the Coorgs of South India*, Oxford University Press, London, 1952, and *Social Change in Modern India*, University of California Press, Berkeley, 1966.

[34] M. Galanter, "The Religious Aspects of Caste: A Legal View," in D. Smith (ed.), *South Asian Politics and Religion*, Princeton University Press, 1966.

[35] W. Norman Brown, "The Content of Cultural Continuity in Asia," in *Journal of Asian Studies*, 20, August 1961; Harold A. Gould, "The Adaptive Functions of Caste in Contemporary Indian Society," in *Asian Survey*, 3, September 1963; J.R. Gusfield, "Tradition and Modernity: Misplaced Polarities in the Study of Social Change," in *American Journal of Sociology*, 72, January 1967; and K. Ishwaran (ed.), *Change and Continuity in India's Villages*, Columbia University Press, New York, 1970.

[36] Milton Singer, "The Social Organization of Indian Civilization," *op. cit.*

[37] Oscar Lewis, *La Vida*, Vintage Books of Random House, New York, 1966, p. xliii.

[38] *Ibid.*, pp. xlv-xlviii.

[39] *Ibid.*, pp. xlvi-xlvii.

[40] *Ibid.*, p. xlvii.

[41] See Oscar Lewis, "Reply to Valentine," in *Current Anthropology*, 10, April-

June 1969; David Matza, "Reply to Valentine," in *Current Anthropology*, 10, April-June 1969; Charles A. Valentine, *Cultural and Poverty*, *op. cit.*; and "Culture and Poverty, Critique and Counter-Proposals," in *Current Anthropology*, 10, April-June, 1969.

[42] Chennanagar is a pseudonym. It is used to protect the interests of the people in the setting studied. However, in that a particularly interested person could ascertain the real name of this slum, all names of persons given in this study are also pseudonyms.

[43] Charles Stokes, "A Theory of Slums," in *Land Economics*, 48, April 1962.

[44] On the meaningfulness of this procedure see Rosalie Wax, *Doing Fieldwork: Warnings and Advice*, University of Chicago Press, Chicago, 1971.

Two

The City and its Slums

THE CITY

Historical Sketch

When the British first came as traders to South India they established themselves to the north of Madras.[1] Looking for a satisfactory
place in which to locate a factory, the East India Company successively attempted to set up trading posts at Pulicat, Masulipatam, and
Armagam, with only marginal success. It found the Dutch unfriend-
ly neighbours at the first step. At all three places it found it difficult
to establish effective trade relations with the Indians. Thus, in
1639, Francis Day, the chief of the Armagam factory, set out in
search of a new trading location. The place he found was an un-
inspiring tract of land. Yet on this site, that same year, he founded
Fort St. George and here Madras developed.

The histories of the Fort are interesting.[2] On the one hand, the
Fort was a storm centre in South India. It was taken by the French
in 1746, and returned to the English in accord with the treaty of
Aix-la-Chapelle in 1749. It served as the supply base for the
campaigns against the French at Pondicherry and saw, in 1761,
the fortifications and public buildings from which the Frenchman
Dupleix had hoped to rule India south of the Krishna river laid to
ruins.[3] During the last forty years of the seventeenth century,
it was unsuccessfully attacked twice by Hyder Ali of Mysore and
twice by his son, Tippu Sultan.

On the other hand, the Fort served as the nucleus around which the
city developed. It protected the trading interests of the British as
Madras became the great market not only for the cotton materials
that formed the staple of the exports to Europe, but also for every

type of merchandise bought or sold along the coasts of South India. It gained rapidly in prestige, within eighteen months of its founding becoming "the chief British settlement in Hindustan and the principal port for European and native goods."[4] Madras later lost   its commercial pre-eminence to Bombay and Calcutta but today it is still the most important commercial centre in South India.

Patnam in Tamil means a town on the sea coast and the name Madraspatnam is mentioned in the first grant giving the land to the British. Whatever the origins of the name, then, a village so called existed in the vicinity of the Fort even before the arrival of the British.[5] The new town that grew up to the north of the Fort was named Chennapatnam, most probably for the village that earlier existed there.[6] "Whites" — Portuguese from San Thome, Armenians, Jews,   and English—in the   early years settled primarily in and around the Fort and this area came to be called "White Town." Indians settled mostly in the Chennapatnam or "Black Town" area.[7] The English called the combined town Madras, the name they had used from the beginning, while the Indians used the name Chennapatnam.

Madras grew in stages, both in population and in land area, and the company only gradually acquired surrounding   villages.[8] Triplicane was acquired in 1676 in rent from the Sultan of Golconda. In 1693, Elihu Yale, then Governor of Madras, obtained the villages of Egmore, Purasawalkam, and Tondiarpet in rent. These villages, together with Triplicane, came to be known as the "Four Old Towns," and later were taken under the direct control of the Company. The "Five New Villages"—Tiruvottiyur, Nungam-bakkam, Vyasarpady, Kathivakkam, and   Sathangudu — were granted to the English in 1708 by the Moghul Nawab, Daud Khan. In 1742, the British gained from the boy Nawab of the Carnatic, the son of Safdar Ali, the villages of Periamet, Perambur, Pudupak-kam, Ernavore, and Sadayankuppam; and, in 1749, in the name of their ally, Nawab Muhammed Ali of the Carnatic, the British took over the San Thome and Mylapore areas. By the beginning of the nineteenth century the area under the jurisdiction of Fort St. George was nearly the same in extent as the area now under the jurisdiction of the Madras City Corporation.

Population Growth and Development

Madras grew rapidly in population between 1639 and the middle

Table 2.1

ESTIMATES OF POPULATION IN MADRAS CITY 1639-1863

Year	Population	Source of estimate
1639	7,000	East India Company
1646	19,000	East India Company
1670	40,000	Thomas Bowery in *Countries Round the Bay of Bengal* (1670)
1674	50,000	Sir William Langhorne
1683	400,000	Sir Joseph Hearne (Governor of Fort St. George)
1791	300,000	Col. Love in his *Vestiges of Old Madras*
1822	462,051	Government of Madras
1863	1,000,000	Sir Charles Trevylean (Governor of Madras).

Source: S. Chandrasekhar, "Growth of Population in Madras City, 1639-1863," in *Population Review*, vol. 8, no. 1, January 1964, p. 19.

of the nineteenth century, from the time it was no more than a small fishing village to the time it had become a capital city and commercial centre. S. Chandrasekhar, then Director of the Indian Institute for Population Studies, Madras, compiled population growth figures for the city, using available estimates. These are given in Table 2.1.

The Table estimates are not based on careful censuses and cover only the "White" and "Black Town" parts of the developing city. Nevertheless, they are useful approximations and give an indication of the city's pattern of growth.

The all-India Censuses were started in 1871, and from this time on the population figures for the city are more accurate. Decennial population figures for Madras are given in Table 2.2.

Table 2.2

DECENNIAL POPULATION FIGURES FOR MADRAS, 1871-1961

Year	Population	Year	Population
1871	397,552	1931	647,230
1881	405,848	1941	777,481
1891	452,518	1951	1,416,056
1901	509,346	1961	1,729,141
1911	518,660	1970*	2,312,700
1921	526,911		

Source: Adopted from Table 2 in S. Chandrasekhar, *op. cit.*
*Estimate by the Statistics Department, Government of Tamilnadu.

Population figures in Table 2.2 are given for the areas within the jurisdiction of the Madras City Corporation. Because this area has not remained constant, the city's growth in population in part can be explained through the addition of new areas. The area covered by the Corporation in 1871 was 27.60 square miles. By 1931 it had become 29.40 square miles, and in 1946, 49.85 square miles, its present extent. However, the density of population has increased along with the size of the city, increasing almost uniformly from 18,432 per square mile in 1901 to 34,707 per square mile in 1961. It continues to increase today.[9]

The growth of population in Madras has resulted from natural increase as well as from migration into the city. Table 2.3 gives figures that identify the relative importance of these two factors for the census years of the first sixty years of this century.

In the first two decades identified in Table 2.3, deaths exceeded births, due largely to the poor health conditions that prevailed in the city during this period. Since that time, however, the situation has changed. Chandrasekhar explains things thus:

In the Indian context the death rate has been the decisive factor in deciding the magnitude of natural increase. There has been a steady decline in the death rate of Madras. Since 1951 this decline has been definitive and almost dramatic: the death rate has been almost halved from 29.31 in 1951 to 16.15 in 1962. The birth rate, on the other hand, has remained more or less constant, around 40 per 1000 during 1901-61..... With a constant birth rate and steadily declining death rate, the rate of natural increase has been gradually increasing over the years.[10]

Meanwhile, between 1901 and 1961, immigration accounted for about two-thirds of the population increase in the city (see Table 2.3), and both "push" and "pull" factors help account for this.[11] The periodic failures of the monsoons and subsequent crop failures, the oft-noted surplus of labour in the agricultural sector and the revolutions that characterize farming techniques in the country, leading often to the economic and social displacement of certain rural groups, have served to push the unemployed, underemployed and needy to the cities. Conjointly, the industrial, commercial, educational and cultural offerings of the city have attracted many, for in a

Table 2.3

DECENNIAL POPULATION FIGURES FOR MADRAS SHOWING INCREASES DUE TO
NATURAL INCREASE AND IMMIGRATION, 1901-1961

Period	Total increase	Natural increase	Increase due to migration	Total increase	Percentage increase due to	
					Natural increase	Migration
1901-1911	9,314	−27,470	36,784	1.8	−5.4	7.2
1911-1921	8,251	−22,020	30,271	1.6	−4.3	5.9
1921-1931	120,319	1,687	118,632	22.8	0.3	22.5
1931-1941	227,954	47,367	180,587	35.2	6.1	29.1
1941-1951	540,872	91,543	449,329	61.8	6.5	55.3
1951-1961	309,160	281,904	27,256	21.8	16.3	5.5

Source: Adapted from Tables 5 and 7 given in S. Chandrasekhar, *op. cit.*

general way, the whole of South India lies within the hinterland of Madras.

The planning area to which Madras belongs is the Madras Metropolitan Area, a unit defined by the Tamilnadu Directorate of Town Planning.[12] This area covers roughly 450 square miles — the 49.85 square miles now under the jurisdiction of the City Corporation, plus four municipalities, two townships, and 318 villages — and like other metropolitan areas in the state, has been set aside for special planning consideration. It is now estimated that whereas the population in the Madras Metropolitan Area in 1971 came to about 3.15 million, in 1981 it will come to some 4.149 million, and in 1991 to 5.34 million.[13] With growth figures like these for urban areas throughout the state, city and state officials clearly recognize that planning is essential if the balanced development of the state's cities is to be realized.

Madras Today

Madras is the largest city in India's southern region. Its population is more than twice as large as South India's other great cities—Hyderabad and Bangalore—and its importance as a commercial centre is clearly recognized. Its harbour handles a significant proportion of the country's imports and exports. Its railways and road systems link it with all of the major cities of India.

Until the period of states reorganization in 1956, Madras was the administrative capital of the entire Madras Presidency, an area extending to the southern tip of the country from the southern borders of Orissa and including what is now Tamilnadu as well as parts of Andhra Pradesh, Mysore, and Kerala. Most of Tamilnadu's administrative offices are still located in the city. So also are the various local offices of the Government of India and, of course, the offices of the City Corporation and Madras District (the city is also one of the state's districts).

J.C. Molony, on becoming the president of the Madras Municipal Corporation in 1914, commented that Madras never was and probably never would be a great industrial centre in that it lacked two essential commodities: coal within easy reach and a sufficient water supply on the spot.[14] In fact, Madras has developed industrially far more slowly than have Bombay and Calcutta though it was the chief locale of British activity in India before these cities. But Molony's remark would hardly be applicable today for Madras has certainly taken on an industrial character. Madras District and the surrounding Chingleput District in 1965 accounted for 48.6 per cent of all registered factory employment in the state, and between 1962 and 1965 the figures for registered factory employees in these two districts rose consistently from 78,140 to 178,144.[15] The breakdown of figures for 1951 and 1961 by area of employment (given in Table 2.4) similarly reveals that industrial and related activities account for more and more workers in the city.

Furthermore, industrial estates have developed in many sections of the metropolitan area—for example, at Guindy, Ambattur, Madhavaram, Vyasapady, and Tiruvotiyur—and both public and private sector projects have been strongly encouraged. Among the other larger scale industries Madras has recently introduced are those that involve the production of transport equipment, electrical machinery and appliances, basic metals and metal products, and chemicals and chemical products including rubber, petroleum, and petro-chemicals.

Table 2.4

SECONDARY AND TERTIARY SECTOR EMPLOYMENT BY SUB-GROUPING AND PER CENT, MADRAS CITY, 1951 AND 1961

Subgroup	% of working population	
	1951	1961
Agricultural (excluding mining)	10.9	9.7
Manufacturing (including mining)	22.8	31.7
Commerce and trade	19.5	15.4
Transport	7.8	9.7
Services	39.0	33.5

Source: Tamilnadu Directorate of Town Planning, *Interim Plan—Madras Metropolitan Area*, 1970-71, p. 22.

No matter how industrialized the city has become, though, it retains a slower pace of life than do some of the other great cities in India. C.W. Ranson observed this to be so, saying that the South Indian seems to take more kindly to city life than most of his fellow countrymen. He explained this in part with reference to the relative importance of Adi-Dravidas (literally, ancient Dravidians; officially, members of the Depressed Castes) in Madras. His reasoning went as follows:

This community (the Adi-Dravida) provides the bulk of the manual labour in Madras, and occupies a more prominent place in the life of the city than the 'outcaste' in Bombay and Calcutta. Adi-Dravida migration to Madras is frequently family migration, as opposed to the industrial migration in other centres, which is largely confined to men. The Madras Adi-Dravida tends to establish himself in the city in mud and thatch huts and to retain his own form of community life, within the larger city community. The transition of a family from village life to an Adi-Dravida hutting ground in Madras is much less violent and confusing than the removal of an individual labourer from his village to a 'busti' or 'chawl' in Calcutta or Bombay.[16]

Whether or not such an explanation can find substantive support, it is at least true that the industrial development of Madras has been gradual. And perhaps, because of this, the differences between rural and urban life in this part of India have been less marked than in other areas.[17] More than most cities, Madras did develop in the simple annexation of villages and for a long time was little more than a collection of villages under the jurisdiction of the English centered in the Fort. Furthermore, open spaces and groves of trees have always been a part of the city and, even today (see Table 2.5), the city has large tracts of vacant lands (accounting for 15 per cent of the city's area) and lands used for agricultural and other non-urban purposes (amounting to 12.4 per cent of the city's area).

But Madras is by no means now a simple collection of villages. The various forms of the mass media wield the people together in countless ways. So too do such things as the job market, the opportunities for education and the activities of political parties. And so too do the city's systems of transportation for, like other modern cities, Madras today would be parlayzed without its systems of public conveyance. This is made obvious by the fact that many more than a million fares a day are collected from the people who ride the city's trains and buses.[18]

About 1900, Rudyard Kipling likened Madras to a "withered beldame," dreaming of ancient fame and better days.[19] J.C. Molony, responding to this metaphor thirty years later, defended Madras, calling it "...the pleasantest dwelling place in the East."[20] By now, neither description would easily apply. The city's big roads—the Poonamallee High Road, Mount Road, the Calcutta Trunk

Table 2.5
MADRAS CITY LAND USE 1964

	Percentage to total area	Percentage to developed area
Residential	33.4	38.1
Commercial	3.2	3.7
Industrial	3.8	4.3
Public and semi-public	10.6	12.1
Open spaces	3.4	3.9
Utility and services	0.9	1.0
Transport and communication	17.3	19.7
Vacant lands	15.0	17.2
Non-urban uses	12.4	—

Source: Adapted from Interim Plan—Madras Metropolitan Area, op. cit.

Road, and the South Beach Road, all radiating out from the centre of the city—are often congested with ever increasing volume of every kind of traffic—ranging from wandering water buffaloes to handpulled rickshaws, ox-bundies, bicycles, and heavy trucks.

Traffic accidents are up in every category. Overcrowding on public conveyances at peak periods of the day ranges from 150 to 400 per cent of carrying capacity,[21] and in many of the bazaar areas the movement of traffic is often obstructed. Uncleared heaps of rubbish abound. Pavement dwellers—atleast 15,000 in 1970[22] —clutter the roads in places with their dilapidated shelters, and pose health and traffic problems. Slums, described as they have been by Rama Aranganal, then Chairman of the Tamilnadu Slum Clearance Board, as places "...with gutters streaming around, swarms of mosquitoes invading, herds of pigs roaming about, heaps of filth and garbage scattered all around,"[23] hardly add to the beauty of city. If ever it was, Madras is no longer the "pleasantest place in the the East."

On the other hand, the existence of such problems in itself identifies the life of the city and its continued resurgence. In ways, Madras is physically decrepit, and many immigrants and long-term residents live here under difficult conditions. Yet many people still come to the city with great hopes, and most of the people in Madras find here offerings in music, economic opportunities, cinemas, processions, market places, temples and so forth, a diversity impossible to find in rural areas and a diversity that undermines the interests many have in returning to rural areas. Then too, Madras retains a natural beauty in its setting and, as a city, has many delightful sections.

Climatic and Geographical Setting

Upon returning to Madras in 1938 after an absence of a number of years, Bishop Stephen Neill claimed:

> The South Indian skies are the most beautiful in the world....Those skies never have that hard sapphire brilliance that oppresses the human spirit. There is never in the sunlight that bleaching quality that takes the colour out of all things and reduces them to a general dullness. Nearly always the radiance is tempered by clouds drawn up from the sea by the burning heat; everything stands out clear and bright in its own colour.[24]

Such a description fits in a way. For most people, however, it would hardly be accurate. The British found Madras a place where "timber rots and gun-powder decays with great rapidity unless protected by unusual care."[25] And S. Y. Krishnaswamy, a South Indian novelist, says the climate of Madras deserves independent description "in language used by the poets for high tragedy."[26]

In fact, the climate of Madras is fairly equable, though at times combinations of temperature and humidity make it quite unpleasant. The mean temperature for the coolest months (December and January) is about 76°F, for the hottest months (May and June) about 90°, and for the year about 83°. The annual rainfall of about forty inches falls mainly during the north-east monsoon months of November and December, and to a lesser extent during the period of the southwest monsoon, from the end of June through the middle of September.

The site of Madras (18°15' E. and 13°4' N.) is uniformly level and nowhere rises more than forty-eight feet above sea level.[27] It lies for about ten miles along the coast of the Bay of Bengal, extending inland in a jagged semi-circular fashion. Its soil is a red loam that gives way to a considerable body of sand along the coast. The Cooum River divides Madras into two nearly equal parts. The Adyar River flows through the southern part of the city and the Buckingham Canal — a channel running from the Krishna River in the north to near Pondicherry in the south—passes through Madras parallel to the coast.

SLUMS

Definition and Number

The Commissioner of the Madras Corporation in 1961 discussed the problem of slums in Madras. He said:

According to us, a slum is taken to mean hutting areas with squalid surroundings. In such areas, huts are erected in a haphazard manner without proper access. Minimum basic amenities are lacking in these areas. Protected water supply and drainage arrangements do not exist in these areas. Houses are built up in close proximity not allowing free air to get in. The number of persons living in the slums is on the increase every day without restriction and the condition of these areas is worsening day by day. As the population is increasing in the City, not only slums of the above descriptions increase, but the built-up areas, which were once having all facilities of free ventilation and other hygienic conditions also take a turn for the worse and the built-up areas get unduly crowded. A house where six tenants can live with comfort is occupied by more than a dozen and this unhealthy and heavy congestion in the street houses makes the area worse than the hutted slums. So the term 'slum' will also include such dwellings which on account of such over-crowding, dilapidation and lack of ventilation are detrimental to safety, health and social morals.[28]

 This definition, minus the second class of slums—which leaves the definition of slums as simply "those areas in which huts have been put up in insanitary conditions and without proper facilities"— was used in the excellent 1961 Census study of the city's slums.[29] Nevertheless, it is a rather vague definition. First, with the exclusion of the second category of slums, a large number of persons who live under slum conditions are not classed as slum dwellers. Second, the definition does not pertain to the city's street dwellers. Third, the definition almost makes it imperative to define a simple cluster of huts a slum area, no matter how appropriate such dwelling places may be in the Madras setting, no matter what differences exist among the various kinds of hut settlements and no matter how great a proportion of the dwelling places in village India would have to be similarly classified if the definition were to be used.

The advantages of this minimal definition, however, outweigh its disadvantages for at least two general reasons. First, it fits the popular conceptions of a *cheri* or slum area. Second, it matches the definitions that previously have been used, thus making it possible to understand at least partially the development of slums in the city.

Accordingly, there has been a rapid and consistent growth of slums in Madras. The Special Housing Committee appointed by the Corporation in 1933 estimated at that time that there were 189 slums containing 15,942 huts in Madras.[30] In 1953-54 the Corporation counted 306 slums, containing 57,436 families, and a population of 265,000 in the city. In 1961, the Census found 548 slums with 97,851 households and nearly 24 per cent (412,168 persons) of the population.[31] In turn, the president of the City Corporation estimated in 1971 that up to one-third of the people then lived in slum areas.[32] Though such figures are certainly not rigorously comparable, together they identify the increasing magnitude of the slum problem in Madras.

General Characteristics

A general review of slum characteristics in Madras immediately reveals that in most respects slum dwellers are considerably worse off than non-slum dwellers. Most slums are overcrowded. Of 548 slums in 1961, only 50 were served by the city sewage system. Of the rest, 63 were served only by masonry side ditches, 152 only by open earth ditches and the remainder, 283, by no drainage facilities at all.[33] In that many slums are in low lying areas, the problem of drainage is often severe even in dry weather periods. When it rains heavily and for extended periods of time, thousands of huts are flooded.[34] Only about one-third of the slums have public latrines and in these slums one latrine on the average "serves" about 159 families.[35] In many slums, pigs and dogs roam freely, well serving the slum dwellers as scavengers in one sense; in another, adding to the problems of the slum. In most slums, especially in the rainy seasons, stagnant pools of water and filth collect, adding to the general insanitariness. Slum areas have a birth rate 43 per cent higher than non-slum areas, a rate matched in turn by a death rate which is 50 per cent higher.[36]

Slum dwellers are also handicapped by problems of water supply and housing. With the water table as high as it is, well water can easily be obtained in most parts of the city. But such supplies are almost always insanitary and usable only for washing and bathing. For all but the few slums with access to bore wells, the only source of good water is the municipal water supply. And here real problems of shortage exist.

City planners in 1911 predicted the population of Madras in 1961 would come to 660,000 and planned the city's water supply with this projection in mind. Actually, the population passed this mark in the 1930s, and in that the system of water supply has not been basically redesigned in many years, "the people of the city for the last three decades and more have suffered and are still suffering" from the lack of a sufficient water supply.[37] The average daily supply of filtered water increased from 18.8 million gallons in 1931-32 to 37 million gallons in 1968-69; but, with the unplanned for increase in population, the average per capita daily water supply during this same period dropped from 29.03 to 17.0 gallons.[38]

Dramatic plans to restructure the Madras supply of potable water are being considered today.[39] Yet the problem persists, especially in slum areas. About 25 per cent of the city's slums have no water taps.[40] Those that are supplied with taps are often at the ends of supply lines where the pressure is low many times during the day. At such places it is a familiar sight to see long lines of women awaiting their turns to draw. Also, at certain times of the year, when supplies are short, the Corporation shuts off the water during peak hours to keep the mains adequately filled. The average per capita daily supply of water, in any case, is certainly often much lower here than the seventeen gallons mentioned as an average for the city.

In 1933, a general report on the characteristic conditions of the slums in Madras noted the "...hopeless state of most of the dwellings." It described them as follows:

The huts, which are generally made of mud and thatch or of old kerosene tins, are low hovels, without any aperture for light or air except a doorway so small that one has to stoop to enter. The average size is 8 feet by 9 feet, though many are smaller. In some *cheries* the huts are built back to back, or are separated only by the narrowest alleys, with the result that there is overcrowding of the very worst kind. In most cases the houses are so flimsy that they afford no effective shelter either in the monsoon or in the hot weather.[41]

It is still possible to describe similarly many of the dwellings in the slums of Madras and, in fact, the 1961 Census description sounds much like the previous one:

More than 79% of the slum houses are huts. They are of cheap materials of construction and cost less than Rs. 100 and consist of one room only. They are mostly flimsy structures constructed with mud and thatch. They are impermanent and are liable to destruction by fire and heavy rain. The meanest of huts is built with poles and old kerosene tins and canisters beaten flat and nailed across. Such a construction will be unbearable in the summer. A somewhat better type of hut has a thatched roof. The thatched roof made of palm leaves or fronds and at times with a layer of paddy straw spread over is easily combustible and the mud walls sometimes crumble and collapse in the monsoon rains. People who are economically better off have put up tiled roofs resting on mud walls. Some well-to-do people who prefer to live in slums have built pucca houses. However, a typical slum house is built of mud walls with a thatched roof.[42]

According to the government's slum improvement scheme, the recommended size of a hut should be 300 square feet. By this standard, about 80 per cent of the huts in Madras slums are sub-standard. Nevertheless, with the city's housing shortage as it is—and will continue to be[43]— this is, in general, a problem of relatively little concern. More important is the simple need for shelter.

Types and Development

There is no doubt that the slums in Madras are in poor condition. To describe them simply, however, as "festering ulcers," "breeding grounds for diseases and crimes," as some people in public life have, is to make far too glib a description. Different kinds of slums exist and the differences are important. Factory worker slums have sprung up. So also have slums housing the construction workers employed at special construction sites. Many slum dwellers find only unskilled work as coolies or labourers and many slums are occupied predominantely by such persons. In certain parts of the city, servant slums are easily located. The pattern of life, which in India's villages puts certain groups of people into subordinate and service positions vis-a-vis other groups,[44] is to a large extent also a part of city life, especially in South India. A widespread need for servants persists, especially among the upper classes.

Other slums have grown up in the last fifteen to twenty years, as Tamilians, who during the later years of the nineteenth and early years of the twentieth century travelled to Burma and Ceylon for a livelihood, have been forced to return to Tamilnadu and especially Madras. Most of these refugees were forced to leave almost all of their wealth and possessions in their countries of adoption and though they have been assisted in various ways by the governments of India and Tamilnadu, they are now living in relatively poor conditions.

Other kinds of slums also exist. Certain slum areas are almost exclusively inhabited by Muslims. Others have a dominant proportion of Christians. Many slums are populated largely by members of single occupational groups—for example, by scavengers, carpenters, washermen, and so forth. Others, formerly separate little villages — for example, of fishermen—have been incorporated by the expanding city.

The reasons for which the slums have developed are numerous, and in many ways tie in with the reasons for migration to the city. The problem of slums is directly related to the pressures of population growth. Specifically, the reasons differ for the different types of slums, but in general, the reasons for their development in Madras may be summarized as they have been by the City's Corporation. These are the reasons given:

(*i*) Execution of post-Independence development schemes and the consequent demand for labour.

(*ii*) Lack of demand for labour in rural areas. Villagers who do not find gainful work move to the city where they are sure to get some employment or other.

(*iii*) Consecutive failure of monsoons and drought conditions in the villages.

(*iv*) Influx of population after the cessation of the Second World War and consequent acute scarcity for housing accommodation at reasonable rent.

(*v*) Inability of the casual labourers who are daily wage earners to live in street houses paying economic rent.

(*vi*) Lack of civic consciousness and a growing apathy to respect law in their eagerness to encroach and squat on any

open land or road margins.
(*vii*) Desire to occupy any place near the workspot.[45]

Listing these reasons, the 1961 Census for Madras also lists
the following as "causes responsible for the growth of slums," the
general public indifference to the protection of public property, the
indifferent attitudes of many private landowners to the growth of
slums on their lands (many collect a little on the side from the
occupants), and the fear public officials have of taking "any steps that
will result in public agitation."[46]

Directed Change

Considering their magnitude, there has long been a multi-faceted
interest in alleviating the problems of slum dwellers in Madras.
Medical colleges—for example, the Stanley and Government
Medical Colleges—have for about the last two decades been
actively interested in offering medical and social services to indigent
groups. Agencies such as the Madras Christian Council of Social
Service and a variety of Catholic orders have done such things as
construct latrines in the slums and establish homes for orphans,
the elderly, and beggars. Industries have done much for their employees in the way of housing and the provision of facilities. For
example, the Buckingham-Carnatic Mills and the Integral Coach
Factory complexes provide quarters at controlled rates for many of
their workers. Many independently offered social services exist for
the slum dwellers.[47] Simultaneously, an increasing public awareness
of the problem has emerged, encouraging a greater official interest in
the need to tackle the problem.

On the official level, meanwhile, there is a well-defined recognition
of the need for slum clearance, slum rehabilitation and slum prevention. The central government, in addition to its impressive plans
for community development in rural areas, has frequently noted the
need for urban planning and finds clear support for its development
efforts in the Constitution of India as well as in numerous other
documents. Among other agencies with similar interests and
importance, the Ministry for Urban Development, for example,
has taken as its prime task the "planning necessary to bring about
an orderliness into the amorphous...growth which will otherwise
take place in the...towns and metropolitan areas."[48] Such emphasis
have continuously encouraged the states in their own problems of

slum clearance and improvement.

Official town planning in Madras has a history that begins in the early years of this century. It was recognized as necessary in 1910 in relation to the problems that already were clear in other cities and in Madras.[49] It continues today.[50] In fact, by now it has become a matter of political crusade and the D.M.K. state administration now optimistically predicts the city's slums will be cleared by the late 1970s, with the help of central government funds.[51] The clearance and rehabilitation schemes are elaborate and accommodate the expertise of the long involved State Housing Board as well as the newly organized Tamilnadu Slum Clearance Board.

Recognizing the fact that slums are defined in relative terms and thus will probably always be around, as well as the economic and other problems that today confront India, Tamilnadu, and Madras, the anticipated successes of the schemes should be viewed with extreme caution. Then too, unauthorized slums continue to develop in certain suburban areas of the city even as other slum areas are cleared and developed. Nevertheless, the schemes indicate that today the government of Tamilnadu, in relation to the emphasis and activities of town planning in India, takes the problems of its slums with the utmost public sincerity.

REFERENCES

[1] *Imperial Gazeteer of India*, vol. 2 (The Indian Empire), The Clarendon Press, Oxford, 1908.

[2] Mrs. Frank Penny, *Fort St. George, Madras*, Swan Sonnenschien and Co. Ltd., London, 1900; and J. Talboys Wheeler, *Madras in the Olden Times*, 1639-1748, Calcutta, 1878.

[3] *Imperial Gazeteer of India, op. cit.*, pp. 472-473.

[4] Love in C.W. Ranson, *A City in Transition: Studies in the Social Life of Madras*, The Christian Literature Society, Madras, 1938, p. 10.

[5] K.L. Narasimhan, *Madras City: A History*, Rachana, Madras, 1968, pp. 5,9.

[6] *Imperial Gazeteer of India, op. cit.*, p. 457. Narasimhan, *op. cit.* p. 10, claims that when he made the offer of land to Day in 1639, Damarla Ayyappa Nayak wished the town to be named in honour of his father, Chennappa Nayak, and so called the place Chennapatnam. But this explanation seems less satisfactory than the other.

[7] H.V. Lanchester, *Town Planning in Madras*, Constable and Company, Ltd., London, 1918, pp. 86-88.

[8] K.L. Narasimhan, *op. cit.*, pp. 13-14.

[9] S. Chandrasekhar, "Growth of Population in Madras City, 1639-1961," in *Population Review*, 8 January 1964, p. 23.

[10] *Ibid.*, p. 32.

[11] *Ibid.*, pp. 31-35. For further information on the "push" factors involved see G. Dattatri and S.D. Raj, "Urbanization in India: Planning for a Balanced Urban Planning and Structure," mimeographed paper presented at the seminar, "Urban Planning for a Greater India," Dasaprakash Hotel, Madras, 6 July 1967. On the "pull" factors see C.W. Ranson, *op. cit.*, pp. 57-74.

[12] The Tamilnadu Directorate of Town Planning now prepares development plans for the urban areas of the state. The implementation of these plans has begun.

[13] These estimates reflect a "medium" rate of decline in population increase and are based on figures released by the Tamilnadu Bureau of Statistics and reported in the Tamilnadu Directorate of Town Planning 1970-71, mimeographed issue, *Interim Plan: Madras Metropolitan Area*, pp. 13-14. If rates of population increase are alternatively calculated in terms of "fast" or "slow" rates of decline, the figures appropriately will vary, of course.

[14] J.C. Molony, *A Book of South India*, Methuen and Company, Ltd., London, 1926, p. 19.

[15] *Interim Plan: Madras Metropolitan Area, op. cit.*, p. 20. *Tamil Nadu: An Economic Appraisal 1971-72*, a book published under the auspices of the Finance Department, Government of Tamilnadu, substantiates these figures and gives many more details on the economic situation in the state.

[16] C.W. Ranson, *op. cit.*, p. 3.

[17] In ways, urban life in India is continuous with rural life. In other ways, discontinuities exist. On this, see Owen M. Lynch, "Rural Cities in India: Continuities and Discontinuities," in Phillip Mason (ed.), *India and Ceylon: Unity and Diversity*, Oxford University Press, London, 1967. However, the Ranson comment, (*op. cit.*, p. 3), "The South Indian seems to take more kindly to city life than most of his fellow countrymen," seems still to be true.

[18] In 1968, 1,230,000, according to *Interim Plan: Madras Metropolitan Area*, *op. cit.*, p. 67.

[19] Quoted in C.W. Ranson, *op. cit.*, p. 5.

[20] J.C. Molony, *op. cit.*, p. 15.

[21] *Interim Plan: Madras Metropolitan Area*, *op. cit.*, pp. 61-73.

[22] *Hindu*, 20 November 1970.

[23] *Hindu*, 5 January 1971.

[24] Stephen Neill, *The Cross Over Asia*, The Canterbury Press, London, 1948 p. 138.

[25] H. Dodwell, "The History of Madras," *Indian Science Congress Handbook*, Diocesan Press, Madras, 1921, p. 5.

[26] S.Y. Krishnaswamy, *Kalyanis Husband*, Higginbotham's Pvt. Ltd., Madras, 1967, p. 17.

[27] H.V. Lanchester, *op. cit.*, p. 90.

[28] P.K. Nambiar, *op. cit.*, p. 5.

[29] *Ibid.*

[30] C.W. Ranson, *op. cit.*, p. 106.

[31] P.K. Nambiar, *op. cit.*, p. 7.

[32] *Hindu*, 5 January 1971.

[33] P.K. Nambiar, *op. cit.*, p. 111.

[34] *Hindu*, 23 November 1970, reported that 40,000 residents of low-lying slum areas were rendered homeless because of rain on 22 November 1970. Flooding of this severity occurs only during periods of heavy rains, but flooding even of this severity is not especially uncommon. Many slum dwellers live in areas that are often flooded.

[35] P.K. Nambiar, *op. cit.*, pp. 115-116.

[36] *Ibid.*, pp. 17, 26.

[37] O.T. Raghavan, "Water and Sanitation," mimeographed paper presented at the seminar, "Urban Planning for a Greater India," Dasaprakash Hotel, Madras, 6 July 1967, pp. 1-4.

[38] *Interim Plan: Madras Metropolitan Area*, *op. cit.*, p. 91.

[39] *Ibid.*, pp. 90-107.

[40] P.K. Nambiar, *op. cit.*, p. 114.

[41] Quoted in C.W. Ranson, *op. cit.*, p. 116.

[42] P.K. Nambiar, *op. cit.*, p. 96.

[43] *Interim Plan: Madras Metropolitan Area*, *op. cit.*, pp. 76-77.

[44] This pattern commonly has been defined as the "*jajmani* system." More will be said of this system in Chapter 5.

[45] P.K. Nambiar, *op. cit.*, p. 120.

[46] *Ibid.*, p. 121.

[47] The Madras School of Social Work book, *Social Welfare in the Slums of*

Madras, New India Publishers, Madras, 1965, combines an empirical study of welfare programmes in Madras with an understanding of many of the kinds of services that exist. Though weak in presentation, the book identifies the kinds of private and government services available for slum dwellers. See also P.K. Nambiar, *op. cit.*, pp. 140-151.

[48] *Hindu*, 1 May 1970.

[49] H.V. Lanchester, *op. cit.*

[50] For the most recent official statement on the prevention, clearance, and improvement of slums in Tamilnadu, see the *Tamilnadu Government Gazette Extraordinary*, published by authority of the government of Tamilnadu, Madras 15 January 1971, pp. 7-37. For general information, see also the *Hindu*, 5 September 1971.

[51] *Hindu*, 23 December 1970, 5 January 1971, and 6 January 1971.

Three

Chennanagar

Chennanagar is situated in the northern "manufacturing" region of Madras, along the east bank of the Buckingham Canal and north of the Erukancheri Road (see Figure 1). It lies just north-west of the densely populated Mottai and Narayanappa Naicken Garden areas of the city, in an area which still has open tracts of land but one which is rapidly filling with people as the pressures of population and housing continue. Slums—some forty to fifty years old, others just springing up—dot the area and lie to all sides except the western side of Chennanagar.[1] Here, across the Buckingham Canal, the land remains vacant.

Little that is physically attractive characterizes the immediate Chennanagar setting. The *nagar* itself is built on an old garbage dump that was overlaid with a thin layer of dirt and ashes when it was settled, and the land to all sides is still used for dumping by the city. Trucks regularly pull in with their loads. So too do the ox and water buffalo-drawn carts operated under the auspices of the Municipal Corporation. The loads of refuse are used as land fill, but containing as they do everything from the sweepings of the streets to night soil, and hotel and eating place leftovers, they add to the odours and filth of the area. Small herds of pigs forage around. Rodents abound. The Buckingham Canal—shallow anyway in this part of its course—serves primarily as a sewage canal for the people who live along its banks. Flat boats still ply the canal, transporting firewood, shells, and other bulk commodities into the city, but the traffic that formerly made it meaningful as a transportation artery has largely subsided.

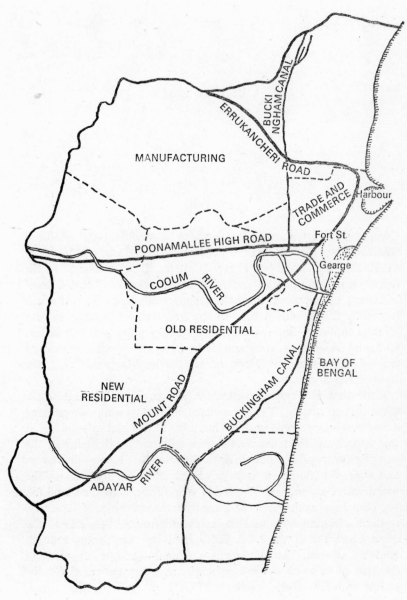

Fig. 1. Madras city.

Being one of the developing sections of Madras, the Chennanagar area knows the kinds of shortages earlier listed for slums. Supply lines bring electricity into most of the surrounding slums. But, for example, the quality of education provided in the area's schools is uniformly poor and many of the area's roads are still not metal-surfaced. Most of those who work here work as labourers or in manufacturing. Relatively few have jobs in such areas of employment as trade and commerce, transport and communication, and construction.[2] Most adults are employed but even the most cursory acquaintance with the area is enough to make the observer aware of the poverty and the high rates of underemployment.[3]

Moving In

Settlers first tried to move into Chennanagar in the early spring of 1966. At this time some of the D.M.K. party leaders in the nearby Washermenpet area, hearing that the Congress party was encouraging some of its supporters to move on and claim unoccupied government and corporation lands, encouraged some of its own supporters to move on to the land on which Chennanagar now stands. The houses the first settlers erected were twice torn down by the police under clearance notices signed by the Congress mayor. The settlers, under the advice of their Washermenpet leaders, then awaited the anticipated election of a D.M.K. leader to the position of mayor. When one was elected later that year, they again tried to settle the land and this time were not evicted. Ashish Bose points out that political parties often play a game in helping the disadvantaged, profiting later through their support.[4] On the one hand, the Chennanagar people were assisted by the D.M.K. and in response have always supported this party.[5]

On the other hand, association with the D.M.K. have also profited the Chennanagar people.[6] Upon the strong encouragement of members of the D.M.K.—now in political control in the city as well as the state—Chennanagar was settled with careful regard for the outlay of streets and housing plots, and thus with a view to permanence that has encouraged the orderly development of the slum. Furthermore, in an official survey taken in 1970, the corporation, by its actions, has indicated the land will continue to be a residential area even though it was settled illegally.

Thus, though the settlers probably will never gain deeds to the land despite their best efforts, they will continue to benefit in a number of additional ways. In simple economic terms, for one thing, the people have not even had to pay rent since they moved. For another, for the Rs 2 each settling family had to pay to obtain "rights" papers to its twenty by thirty foot plot, plus the Rs 12.50 required of each plot owner for road laying, each family now has "squatters" rights to its land and, in effect, a permanent place to call its own. Resettlement or other developments may some day take place, displacing at least some of the people. However, the chances are that many of them will never have to leave. Even if they must, on the other hand, their chances are that in the process, in these days, the government will resettle them in permanent housing quarters. Meanwhile, the people can rent their property if they choose, sell their "rights" to their plots and so forth.

In other terms also, the move to Chennanagar has paid off for the people for they have here achieved for themselves a measure of social and political stability. The *nagar* is more and more becoming a permanent little residential community in and of itself.

The people who settled Chennanagar came from many different parts of the city and from some rural areas. But most of them (64 per cent) came from the crowded and neighbouring areas around Old Washermenpet. Some came because they were literally crowded out of their old localities. Many made the move because they could not afford even the small monthly rents (commonly between Rs 7 to 15 per family) they previously had been required to pay. Others came for a combination of reasons, taking into additional consideration such prospects as the possibility that land claimed in this way would eventually become their own. The leaders of the new settlement recognized their successes here would probably serve well their own political interests in the long run. For whatever reasons the people came, however, when it became clear they would not again be evicted, the land was quickly claimed by the number of household units appropriate to the number of outlined plots.

The leaders most aware of the chance to claim the land made sure their friends and supporters had a chance to find a plot. Otherwise, the move to occupy Chennanagar was not controlled and did not occur along any of the lines—for example, those of caste, language, and region—that in traditional India commonly mark off groups of people from each other. Telugus as well as Tamils, Harijans as well as a few of the "twice-born" castes, and the very poor as well as the not-so-poor all found plots largely on the basis of whether or not they got there while land was still available. By the end of 1966, the 408 plots that make up the *nagar* had all been claimed and registered under the guarantee of local political leaders. One plot only was registered in the name of a single nuclear family.

Living Conditions
The streets of Chennanagar are systematically arranged (see Figure 2) and like the *nagar* itself are named after leading figures of the Dravidian movement. The *nagar's* houses are numbered according to plot and, in all, there are now 376 occupied houses here. Houses have not yet been built on some of the plots, others are taken up by a public latrine and a local political association building. Seven houses have collapsed and are not occupied.

All but six of the Chennanagar houses have low mud walls and thatch roofing. The six different houses have masonry walls and roofs of either asbestos sheeting or tile. One of the latter houses covers parts of three lots and houses a joint family consisting of three nuclear families. Otherwise, all the Chennanagar houses are confined to their own plots of land.

The typical Chennanagar house is about fourteen by ten feet in dimensions. It commonly has a small hole in one wall that serves as a window, and a doorway that can be closed with a wooden or thatch door. Its floor and walls are surfaced with a mixture of cow-dung and dirt and a similar mixture surfaces the area by the doorway. Just as in rural India, this mixture serves well when it is carefully applied and periodically touched up. It is cheap, and when dry, provides for an easily cleaned and hard surface. A little cooking area can commonly be found in one corner of the Chennanagar hut, the family's religious centre, with pictures of some of the favoured deities in another. The thatch roof commonly leaks in the heaviest rains but most of the time gives adequate shelter. The Chennanagar hut represents an investment of about Rs 300; the roof costs about Rs 150, the rest of the house the balance.

The possessions of the majority of the people are simple and few in number. Several clay cooking utensils and polished brass water containers may be found in the cooking corner. Many of the people have a simple bed with a wooden frame and a surface woven with a cheap quality rope. Clothing usually hangs from one or more of the rafters. The bedding and thatch matting the family uses is bundled along a wall, perhaps on the metal or wooden trunk in which the family

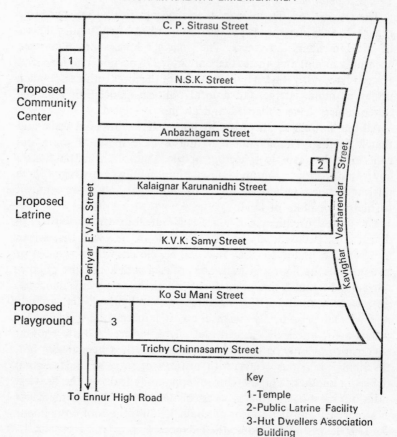

BUCKINGHAM CANAL

CHUNAM KALAVAI-LIME KILNAREA

C. P. Sitrasu Street

1

Proposed
Community
Center

N.S.K. Street

Anbazhagam Street

2

Kalaignar Karunanidhi Street

Proposed
Latrine

K.V.K. Samy Street

Ko Su Mani Street

Proposed
Playground

3

Trichy Chinnasamy Street

Periyar E.V.R. Street

Kavighar Vezharendar Street

To Ennur High Road

Key

1-Temple
2-Public Latrine Facility
3-Hut Dwellers Association
   Building

Fig. 2. Outline of streets in Chennanagar.

stores most of its other material posessions. Three or four families have transistor radios, twenty-five families own bicycles. The households with people engaged in a "household industry" also have at least the minimum facilities their particular interests imply.

With the average household consisting of five to six members, the Chennanagar huts are relatively crowded when all of the family members are indoors. But, with the weather as it is most of the time, this crowding is not too often a problem for, as in much of the rest of India, much of the activity of life takes place out-of-doors. Those who make cloth operate their shuttles in their huts or in thatch shelters attached to their huts. They often work outside when they card and spool thread, and, of necessity, set up their straightening apparati in the streets for the pieces of cloth they weave are usually ten to fifteen yards in length. Similarly, those who roll *beedis* (leaf rolled "cigarettes"), repair boxes or pursue other household activities, work in their huts if necessary, outside if the weather permits. During the hot season, many of the Chennanagar people sleep outside. At all times of the year it is more natural to find informal visiting groups of men and women outside than in. Children are seldom restricted to their huts.

A number of persons, journalists in particular, have observed that in India there often appears to be a great emphasis on personal hygiene and cleanliness but a public disregard for the same. Some of these persons tie their ideas in with the notion that since the social organization of Indian civilization is hierarchically arranged in accord with the principles of caste and according to underlying notions of inequality, a basic disregard for the welfare of others exists.

Whatever the merits of such considerations, there is an obvious difference between the cleanliness of public and private places in Chennanagar. But the reasons here are not so much due to some hypothesized disregard for the rights of others as to a combination of other factors. In relation to the many shortages the people experience, they are forced to make do with what little they have. With almost no latrines available, adults relieve themselves in the open areas that surround the *nagar*. Children are permitted to relieve themselves where they will. That the basis on which Chennanagar rests and the surrounding areas have served as municipal garbage dumps adds to the problem of local sanitation. Twenty lime kilns lie along the Buckingham Canal on the Chennanagar side (see

Figure 2). When there is no wind or when it blows away from Chennanagar, these kilns provide no difficulties. On the other hand, when the wind comes from the west, bits of chalk dust hang in the air, descending on Chennanagar like snow. The streets are full of dirt and in the hot season lie heavy in dust, in the wet season deep in mud. Banana stalks, cocoanut husks, and bits of wood are picked out of refuse piles and dried in the streets to be used in fires. Cow-dung patties made of mixtures of dung, grain husks, and bits of straw dry where they are placed on the sides of houses or along the streets. These too are used for fuel. Pieces of paper are collected for wrapping and for starting fires.

Considering such things, in fact, it is surprising not that there is as much filth as there is in the streets and public places of Chennanagar, but that the Chennanagar people keep themselves and their huts as carefully as many of them do. Most dress carefully when they need to. Women make lime-chalk designs on the hard surfaces in front of their huts, especially during festival seasons. Many families have at least one little carefully tended flowering tree near their houses. And many people plant little gardens. Some of the occupied huts are poorly kept and are on the verge of collapsing. Others have so many leaks in their roofs, they provide almost no shelter during rains. But the physical conditions of life the people experience are due more to the shortages they know than to such factors as "slum mentalities" or the characteristics of the social system to which they belong.

Water

The problems of Chennanagar become even more clear with an analysis of the local supply of water. The Buckingham Canal runs right by the slum and a few of the people have dug shallow wells for themselves. But for reasons already clear, the water from these sources is very impure. It can be used only for gardening, and even the livestock will not drink it. For drinking and bathing water and for water to be used in the washing of clothes, the people must rely on that supplied by the Corporation.

Because there are no taps in Chennanagar, some women walk to taps in neighbouring *nagars* and carry back their filled vessels on their heads and hips. Some of the adolescent boys make round trips to relatively less used public taps with as many as six brass water containers fastened to their bicycles. At least one vendor comes around with an ox-drawn cart carrying a tank of water for sale to those who want to pay the 10 p. he charges per bucket. To avoid the usual lines at the public taps, he fills his water tank during the night. Most of the people, however, get their water from the two local water tanks—each of which holds about 600 gallons and was initially installed at the expense of the Chennanagar people—daily filled by the Corporation.

Necessary as the introduction of a water supply was, it was not a simple response to the needs of the people. Rather, like the process involved in the settlement of the *nagar*, it ties in with political considerations. One tank was installed shortly after the *nagar* was settled, under the patronage of the D.M.K. leaders who encouraged the settlement. This tank is filled twice a day through the authority of the Corporation, its supply distributed under the supervision of the largest local political association.

The other tank was installed in 1969, in relation to the efforts of a dissident local group that gained the patronage of the Congress ward councillor. This association, like the larger one, has D.M.K. interests. But in the local context of scarcity, it turned for support to the area's Congress leadership and gained it. The local Congress leaders received some bribe money and some local political support in the process. The new association gained its own supply of water, enabling it to meet more effectively the threat the larger association had made concerning the possibility that it would withdraw water drawing privileges from the dissidents. The tank of the dissidents is filled once a day.

In all of this, it is obvious that a "politics of scarcity" is operative. And the leaders of the existing political associations enjoy the power and influence that comes out of their ability to control the supply of an item as valuable and scarce as water. Indeed, in this D.M.K. *nagar* the seven households with Congress voting preferences are not permitted to draw water locally. They hope to find the political patronage that will eventually enable them to set up their own water supply. But, for the time being, it is difficult for them locally to remain vocal supporters of the Congress, in practical terms.

The Chennanagar people can help assure the daily delivery of water (*i*) through the influence their political patrons are in a position to exert, and (*ii*) in the daily tip of Rs 1 and the cup of tea they give the tank truck drivers. But with 280 members in the larger political association and more than 100 in the other—some have overlapping memberships, for obvious reasons—no household gets more than four or five gallons a day from local Corporation sources. The situation is not so bad in the cooler seasons of the year. On the other hand, when the weather is hot or the supply is not delivered, for any of a number of reasons, the people are clearly forced to suffer.

Features and Services

A drive along any of the roads that lead out from the centre of Madras is enough to impress most visitors to the city with the richness and diversity of local life. Certainly this is the case for a drive along the Wall Tax Road that leads from the Central Station area up towards Basin Bridge, then becoming the Ennur High Road which passes within a quarter of a mile of Chennanagar. Especially in the mornings and evenings, this road is congested with all kinds of traffic. Buses, trucks, and taxis weave in and out of the slower moving bicycles, carts, and rickshaws. In the mornings the sidewalks and sides of the streets are filled with people going to work, pavement dwellers putting their belongings together, people washing themselves near the public taps, dogs and other animals moving in and out, and rickshaw pullers trying to find their first clients of the day. Little food hotels, trinket shops, and repair shops of every type carry on their businesses from their cramped quarters bordering directly on the sidewalks. Deities in the temples along the way attract at least a passing act of devotion from some of their devotees. Piles of refuse in many places cause the traffic to slow down and often result in an even greater congestion than is otherwise typical. In the evenings the cinema crowds congregate. Throughout the day the hustle and bustle of life is everywhere apparent and only during the nights does the traffic subside. In this as in other parts of the city, hospitals, schools, industries, warehouses, stations, and markets can be found.

Chennanagar does not provide too great a variety in its own round of activities. It is a relatively new community consisting quite uniformly of poor people living in similarly constructed huts. Yet the Chennanagar people are obviously involved in the variety of life the city represents in many different ways. Most of the men daily visit other parts of the city in relation to their work or other activities and all of the Chennanagar people have visited many parts of Madras. Almost no mothers now give birth to their children at home. Instead, they commonly are delivered in nearby public and private hospitals and though, at times, the women complain that they are not treated well in the hospitals and that they have to pay bribes to gain various services, almost all of them very willingly go. So too do the sick and injured. Public health officials, family planning employees and others come into Chennanagar bringing with them their own emphasis and, in turn, making the local people more aware of the kinds of things for which they are eligible. In almost every way, Chennanagar is served by what the city has to offer.

At the same time, Chennanagar has more and more services and facilities of its own. Six of its road intersections now have electric light poles and electric home lighting will soon be accessible to those who can afford it. One man locally sells kerosene. Three families operate little tea and "tiffin" stalls. Four other families sell vegetables, matches, salt, and various cooking ingredients in their own small shops. The *nagar* has its own temple and employs a priest. It hopes eventually to get the Corporation to put in a school and already provides some night classes under the supervision of its local self-help associations. A telephone links its leading political association building with the outside, and though few people use the telephone (the charge is 10 p. per call), it gives the leaders of Chennanagar a little more accessibility to the more powerful leaders they know.

At various times—for example, when the *nagar* was founded and when new facilities are installed — the people have successfully gotten together in inviting important persons to come and enjoy with them their successes. Vendors now come around more and more regularly, increasingly coming to define Chennanagar as one of their own special sales areas. So too do tinkers and others with their special abilities to do such things as resurface cooking utensils and fix leather objects.

Chennanagar now has its first public latrine and will soon have another. The latrines are being provided by the Madras Christian Council of Social Service at a cost of Rs 15,000 per unit and each unit contains six bathing stalls, six toilets and its own deep water well and pump facility. In its own right, Chennanagar now also receives assistance in the form of various needed commodities and in the guarantee of help in times of special emergencies from the Madras Christian Council of Social Service and from other public and private agencies.

THE PEOPLE

One of the Chennanagar self-help associations owns two carom boards and several of the men own decks of cards. Otherwise, there are few formal recreational facilities.

Yet, of course, there are many ways in which the Chennanagar people entertain themselves and there is much that interrupts the drabness of local life. Children play with things they salvage from dump piles or, like children almost anywhere else, with mud cakes, tin cans, and the like. Small boys fashion tops and kites for themselves or purchase the cheapest makes available. They play many varieties of tag and marbles. Young men play carom together in the evenings and on holidays, sometimes placing small bets on the outcomes of a contest but usually playing just for fun. All of the people know many simple games requiring little or no equipment. Groups of men often gather in the evenings to drink fermented palm juice or liquor and to talk together. From time to time, fights and arguments —sometimes serious enough to involve the use of glass, knives, and sticks as weapons, but usually with much more "bark" than "bite" —break out.

Most of the young men enjoy the cinema and attend whenever they can, perhaps averaging two or three movies a month. Older men go less frequently and few women go at all. Until the age of puberty, girls locally play where they will, with few restrictions. After puberty and until marriage, they generally remain close to their homes, going out only in the company of other members of their families.

Trips to temples and pilgrimage centres have recreational as well as religious meaning for most of the people. Visits by special outsiders are often eagerly anticipated and long remembered. The periodic appearances in Chennanagar of travelling minstrels and acrobats, and people with manually operated ferris wheels and merry-go-rounds are happily viewed by many, especially the children. Special events in the calendar year, special occasions in the life cycles of individuals, political campaigns, and so forth, attract much attention.

Distribution by Age, Sex, and Literacy

In Madras, as in most other cities of India[7] (*i*) there are more males than females in most adult age categories, and (*ii*) literacy rates are generally higher for males than for females. Table 3.1 gives relevant figures from the 1961 Census for Madras.

Table 3.1

DISTRIBUTION OF MADRAS POPULATION BY SEX, AGE, AND LITERACY

Age group	Persons	Total population		No. of illiterate	
		Males	Females	Males	Females
0-4	228,927	115,854	113,073	115,854	113,073
5-9	213,553	108,419	105,134	32,928	38,456
10-14	183,919	94,676	89,243	9,870	18,355
15-19	149,676	73,859	75,817	10,114	23,824
20-24	185,546	96,714	88,832	13,407	35,609
25-29	176,541	91,333	85,208	16,082	40,607
30-34	137,920	75,725	62,195	14,594	31,340
35-44	210,543	121,662	88,881	27,987	50,618
45-59	171,211	95,841	75,370	25,189	47,613
60+	71,132	35,517	35,615	10,406	24,769
A.N.S.*	173	101	72	67	53
Total	1,729,141	909,701	819,440	276,498	424,317

Source: Census of India, 1961.
*Age not stated.

The preponderance of males in Madras is largely due to the migration of adult males to the city from rural areas. The males come in search of employment, later sending for other members of their families if they are successful. The differences in rates of literacy reflect the favoured position males have always had in the Indian educational process as well as their greater need for an ability to read and write in relation to their jobs and styles of life.

A breakdown of the population figures for Chennanagar by age and sex (see Table 3.2) shows a greater number of males in all age categories above fifteen years except for the 20-24 and 25-29 categories. However, in all categories here the differences are slight, pointing to the comparative sex balance of the community and the relative absence of excess males. One would expect this, though, for Chennanagar was settled largely by families with their own roots largely embedded in the local urban context, not by families with direct linkages to rural areas and thus families potentially housing a greater number of at least temporarily

Table 3.2

DISTRIBUTION OF CHENNANAGAR POPULATION BY
SEX, AGE, AND LITERACY

Age group	Persons	Total population Males	Females	No. of illiterate Males	Females
0-4	257	125	132	125	132
5-9	242	129	113	80	74
10-14	199	105	94	22	40
15-19	156	84	72	16	35
20-24	155	77	78	19	37
25-29	220	107	113	16	65
30-34	143	73	70	13	48
35-44	188	100	88	51	63
45-59	206	109	97	39	75
60+	84	54	30	33	25
Total	1,850	963	887	414	594

unattached males. Eighteen per cent of the Chennanagar people were born in villages and in small towns in Tamilnadu. Five per cent were born in other cities in South India, the rest in Madras. With respect to literacy, the Chennanagar figures (see Table 3.2) show, as do the figures for Madras and India, in general, that males are far more likely than females to be literate.

Language

The distribution of the Tamilnadu and Madras populations by first language is given in Table 3.3.

Table 3.3

TAMILNADU AND MADRAS POPULATIONS BY FIRST LANGUAGE

Language	Population Tamilnadu	Madras
Tamil	28,011,099	1,226,619
Telugu	3,363,579	244,632
Kanarese	853,211	15,055
Malayalam	399,206	57,924
Other	1,067,858	184,911

Source: Census of India, 1961.

Though Tamil is obviously the principal language of Tamilnadu, there also has long been a large Telugu speaking minority in both Tamilnadu and Madras. The two language regions are contiguous with each other. Madras under the British Raj was the administrative centre for large sections of what is now Andhra Pradesh (the Telugu language state), and many Telugus, in the past, were attracted by the better employment opportunities some of the more industrially and commercially developed centres in Tamilnadu then offered. In Madras, in comparison with the number of people who claim Tamil as their first language, roughly one-fifth as many consider Telugu to be their first language. For sections of northern Madras, sections especially attractive in the past to immigrant Telugu labourers, the proportion is considerably higher.

Seventy-six per cent of the Chennanagar people give Tamil as their mother tongue, 22 per cent give Telugu; of the remainder, nineteen persons give Urdu, twenty persons give Malayalam, and one person considers himself a native speaker of Hindi. All the people of Chenna-nagar speak Tamil fluently and about half are fluent in Telugu. Three or four persons can speak some English but only one can carry on a lengthy and intelligent conversation in English. Fifteen to twenty individuals consider themselves fluent in at least three languages, the usual combination coming from the South Indian languages of Tamil, Telugu, Kanarese, and Malayalam.

Some Biographical Sketches

Age, sex, literacy, and language are some of the general categories according to which the Chennanagar people can be classified. Others will emerge as we proceed. However, the use of categories in analysis, though necessary, often obscures certain more intimate understandings about the ways in which the people live. To counter this, at least in part, included below are simple personal sketches of five of the people. None of the five are any more "average" than are most of the others who live in Chennanagar. But then, neither are any of them particularly unusual.

Tulkhannan's first wife died of "fever" twelve years ago. He now lives with his second wife — displaced from Burma along with other Tamilians during the second world war — and his four young children in a Chennanagar house he rents from a friend at the rate of Rs 5 per month. When he was young, Tulkhannan learned to be a weaver, the hereditary occupation of the caste to which he belongs.

Soon, though, he found the possibility of remaining a weaver undermined as more and more commercially woven cloth appeared on the
market and the demand for traditional materials declined. He next
rolled *beedis*. But this too he soon found unprofitable. Now
Tulkhannan simply sells ice-cream in the Sowcarpet area, using a
cart he rents from a commercial firm and earning Rs 4-5 a day. His
wife and children help him support his family by rolling the thread
used to tie *beedis* together and selling this to *beedi* manufacturers
at a daily profit of 60 n.p.

Now forty-five, Tulkhannan has been a supporter of the Congress
party for the last twenty years. He keeps photographs of Mahatma
Gandhi, Kamaraj Nadar, and other Congress leaders in his home and
feels the Congress councillor of the area ward has served the people
well. Tulkhannan is a member of the Zilla Parishad Congress
Committee for this part of Madras.

Many of Tulkhannan's prospects tie in with his membership in the
Congress party. Having contacts with Congress leaders in the area,
he is in a position to exercise a certain amount of power. He recently
has been successful in helping organize a Congress association in
Chennanagar and now is trying to get a local supply of water for those
who support the Congress party. Meanwhile, he claims that when
Chennanagar people are in trouble—with the police, for example —
they often come to him, asking him to intercede on their behalf with
the Congress councillor.

On the other hand, Tulkhannan's Congress identifications have
also caused him problems. When he first moved to Chennanagar he
claimed a plot of land as did the others, and built a house. Unfortu-
nately for him, his house was washed away in the rains and he was
forced to take shelter in his friend's vacant house next door. To
spite him, the DMK leaders, in turn, allotted his plot of land to
someone else and though Tulkhannan has been trying to get it
back, he has so far been unsuccessful. Another of Tulkhannan's
problems has to do with water. Because he is a Congress supporter,
his wife is not permitted to draw water locally. Instead, she is forced
to fetch it from a railway crossing tap three miles away.

Tulkhannan is more religious than most of his *nagar* fellows. He
occasionally visits temples, he says prayers every morning, and every
Friday his wife performs *puja* (ritual ceremony) in their home. He
claims the existence of a god has often been demonstrated for him,
saying he himself was once cured by God of a sickness the doctors

told him was incurable. He believes in rebirth and says a person must lead a good life in order to be reborn into a higher position in another life. He has taken his family on a pilgrimage to Tirupathi and says he will go again when he can save enough money to afford it. Concerning caste rules, he does not believe it necessary to abide by the dietary rules common to caste, but he considers intercaste marriages to be wrong. He says he tolerates all religious orientations.

Meshack's story is considerably different. Brought up in Madras in a Hindu Harijan family, he became a Christian at the age of fifteen against the wishes of his family. He was first a member of the Vepery Baptist Church. Later he successively took memberships in the Apostolic and Pentecostal Churches. Meshack is now seventy and is retired after thirty years of service in the Madras police force. He lives with his wife and two daughters. His eldest daughter was once married but her husband left her and she no longer knows where he is. The other daughter has studied up to the eighth standard and has lately been looking for a job, without success. She is ready for marriage but Meshack and his wife do not yet have enough money for the kind of dowry they think is necessary to attract a desirable mate. Meshack's two sons both live away from home, one lives in Madras but he never visits Chennanagar and about him Meshack knows nothing; the other lives in Mysore where he works as an upper division clerk earning a salary of Rs 250 per month. The first son is married, the second isn't. When the second son was of a marriageable, Meshack gave him Rs 2,000 with which to get married. Instead, the son invested it in a savings account and now refuses to pay it back.

Meshack, his wife, and his two daughters live on the Rs 25 monthly allowance he gets from his police pension and the proceeds that come from the *vadai* (spicy, fried "doughnut"), *idli* (steamed rice "cake") and other items his womenfolk prepare and sell. Meshack feels caste differences in Chennanagar are seldom observed and claims that though he is a Harijan Christian, he is subjected to little, if any, local discrimination. He reads the Bible and prays regularly. He also attends Christian services from time to time. His daily round of activities begins as it always has at about five in the morning. But he works more slowly now than of late and no longer has much to do. Among his wishes, he would like to get work for his younger daughter, to have his older daughter reunite with her husband, to find more appreciation from his sons, and to obtain the deed to the plot of land on which he lives. Otherwise he seems satisfied. He has a debt of Rs

300 but this he is slowly paying off.

Many of Meshack's recollections have to do with his police career and apparently he was a good officer. He studied on his own through the eighth standard, joined the police at eighteen and underwent training in Vellore. He earned a steady income of up to Rs 90 per month which, together with a side income from the sale of milk and other things along the way, provided him and his family with an adequate standard of living at most times. Some of his recollections of the police context in which he worked are given below.

In my service I came across many different kinds of people. Some were honest, others were not. I was honest, but in police service in Madras it is probably true that only one in a hundred will not take bribes. If you ask a policeman today what a policeman does he will probably tell you the policeman serves the people in protecting them and providing for their security. I agree, and the police are necessary. But policemen also do many evil things. Most people know that the inner meaning for the word police is a 'person as cunning as a jackal.' Once I was offered a position as sargeant but I did not accept it. I knew that in that position I would have to charge-sheet many people incorrectly, record false things about people and punish innocent people because that's what a sargeant has to do. Today the police especially bother the poor people, particularly the rickshaw pullers. Suppose a rickshaw puller parks his rickshaw near the roadside and runs into a hotel to get some coffee or rest, the police immediately try to fine him. The law says the policeman should warn the rickshaw puller first, fine him later if he does not learn. To get away without paying a fine, the rickshaw puller must pay a bribe. The police never treat important people like this.

There is room to challenge some of Meshack's recollections but this is the way he talks of his work in the police force.

Krishnan is fifteen and lives with his father, mother, and three younger brothers and sisters. His mother works as a coolie when she can. His father works in a small private workshop in Padi, about ten miles from Chennanagar. Krishnan's elder brother is employed as a coolie by the Government of India Highways Department at a salary of Rs 3 a day and stays in Guindy. He visits his family about once a month and when he does, gives Krishnan's father Rs 5 or 10 in the way of help.

Krishnan is in the seventh class in the Corporation school in nearby Meenambalnagar. But he does not attend too regularly, often simply loafing around Chennanagar or, when his parents both work, staying home to care for his younger siblings. Krishnan likes mutton and prawn curries and enjoys eating in the little hotels near Chennanagar. Usually, though, he has no extra money and simply shares the evening meal of rice and vegetable curry his mother prepares. He takes no solid food at noon. In the mornings he eats rice left over from the day before. On an average, Krishnan goes to the cinema three times a month and he especially enjoys the adventure films in which the film star M.G. Ramachandran acts.

Like many of his fellows, Krishnan is often restless in Chennanagar and finds little locally to occupy his time. As a result, he has lately taken to roaming around in different sections of Madras and he speaks excitedly of the many attractions of the city. His interests, however, are rather serious in the long run and he expects to pass through both high school and a course in technical training, hoping then to get a job as a factory worker. In practical terms, he looks forward to the day he can own his own bicycle and transistor radio. In other terms, he feels he must learn English now in order to some day best compete in the job market. He practices English with those who are able to help him

Anantamma is sixty years old, semi-invalid, and now living by herself in a ramshackle hut. She can no longer cook for herself or move far from her dwelling. Her hearing is poor and she will die before long. A married daughter who also lives in Chennanagar brings her a little portion of rice and curry water once a day. Otherwise, Anantamma stays alone. All of her possessions would not be worth more than Rs 50.

Anantamma is a Harijan by caste. At fifteen she ran away from her native village in southern Andhra Pradesh with a man of a low level Sudra caste. She never formally married the man but maritally lived with him until his death sixteen years ago. Since she left her village, she has had no ties with the village.

When Anantamma and her husband first came to Madras, he found a job as a sweeper. Later he learned to wash clothes and eventually found a job as a washerman in the Stanley Government Hospital. Anantamma and he first lived in a slum colony of Telugus in Vepery.

From there they moved to Washermenpet. The move to Chennanagar, in turn, represents an investment on the part of Anantamma's daughter and her husband for they will "inherit" her property when Anantamma dies. Anantamma gave birth to five living children but all but the one remaining daughter died during childhood of one sickness or another.

G. Naicker once worked in a small export-import bank in Madras and made ample money to provide for his wife and his family. Today, however, his fortunes are in ruin. His eyesight began to fail in the late 1950s and soon thereafter he was compelled to resign from his banking job. Then his wife died. A business disaster followed from which he has never been able to recover. Venturing independently, he made contact with a European firm that existed only on paper. Shipping an order of hides to what he thought was a reliable market, he invested about Rs 5,000. The hides went to the mailing address and were collected, but Naicker never received the payment he had been promised and was eventually forced into poverty. He lives today with his two youngest daughters in Chennanagar in a hut that gives little shelter from either the sun or the rain. He helped his eldest son get married five years ago. He recently raised Rs 500 for his younger son in order to help him gain a promotion in the Madras Post Office Department in which the son has employment. He explains that if he would not give the money to his son's superiors, his son would not be promoted.

Naicker's perspectives of life are still optimistic and he lives happily with his children. Though he has little to do with his neighbours—he thinks, for example, that they are not the kind of people his children should have to come into contact with — he considers himself fortunate enough to have found the place here that he did. He continues to work hard though he is steadily becoming more physically disabled. On his own, he prepares and markets mango chutneys, rose water, toothpaste, curry powders, nail polish, and other items. The proceeds he earns are meagre for there is plenty of competition from others who make similar items, and the commercial market of mass produced articles of this nature keeps prices at a minimum.

Naicker knows Tamil, Telugu, and English fluently and he can recite and understand Sanskrit poems in depth. He believes fervently in Hindu deities and daily honours them with his attentions and offerings. He is learned and able in terms of the larger context to which he belongs, but he is personally caught in a downward economic spiral from which it seems he will not recover.

REFERENCES

[1] For a general picture of the locations of slums in Madras, see P.K. Nambiar, *op. cit.*

[2] On this see the *Census of India*, 1961, *Madras*, volume 9, Part 10 (3), pp. 20-21. The city divisions referred to are divisions 4-7, 9-10, and 21-25.

[3] The definitions of employment used for Census enumeration purposes are minimal. See *ibid.*, p. 8.

[4] Ashish Bose, "The Process of Urbanization in India: Some Emerging Issues," in Richard G, Fox (ed.), *Urban India: Society, Space, and Image*, Duke University Press, 1970, p. 13.

[5] The real name of Chennanagar combines a name of a former DMK party official with the word *nagar*.

[6] The emergence of the DMK party in Madras, the role of political associations in Chennanagar and related matters are the subject matter of Chapter 6.

[7] N.V. Sovani, *Urbanization and Urban India*, Asia Publishing House, Bombay, 1966, pp. 41-89.

Four

Caste, Family, and Community

The history of Indian civilization can be traced back at least to the second millenium B.C. and, certainly, no attempt can be made here to deal with either its complexity or historical emergence. A brief overview of some of the defining features of Indian social organization, however, will better enable us to understand comparatively the social organization of Chennanagar.

The vast majority of the Indian people live in rural areas (about 80 per cent according to the 1971 Census) and in villages. Most villages are small, with a population of less than about two thousand. They are describable, ideal-typically, as agglomerations of joint families, extended kinship groups, castes, and subcastes.[1]

For our purposes here — and according to the lines John Adams and Uwe J. Woltemade encourage in their base line model of village India — the basic unit of the village social system is either the joint or the extended family:

...the joint family consists of two or more nuclear families whose male heads are close consanguineous kin...sharing the same house, cooking together, holding property in common, and worshipping the same deities (and) extended families consist of a nuclear family with unmarried children and a grandparent or more remote relatives who together remain closely associated with the family head's brothers' families.[2]

Actually, only some of the Indian people live in joint or extended family households at any particular time.[3] At all socio-economic levels and especially among the lower level groups, many live in single member, nuclear family or other kinds of households. Yet the structuring of social life in most parts of rural India presupposes the joint or extended family system, and related families at least live in neighbouring households wherever possible.

A caste,[4] meanwhile, can be considered a regionally defined "homogeneous group, with a common occupation or occupations, (practising) endogamy and commensality."[5] It is an organizational entity whose influence helps to channel the interrelationships among the groups and individuals of which it is comprised.

Kin networks are linked together into castes and, ordinarily, "one has no relatives out of one's caste group, and one's relatives are all within the caste. A part of the caste is a person's actual extended kin and the rest is possible kin."[6] In almost all villages, castes are residentially segregated by living areas.[7]

The capacity of families and castes to mould behaviour is embedded in social considerations. It is also religiously embedded. The structures and functioning of the basic family system can be understood only in the light of Hinduism and its consequences for social behaviour. Similarly, Hinduism and caste go side by side for to be a Hindu one must be a member of a particular caste, and if one belongs to a caste, one is, for all practical purposes, a Hindu.[8] The person who lives according to the moral code of his caste is living rightly while the person who violates it is not: living according to the code is rewarded while its violation is punished, both here and in the hereafter.[9]

Throughout rural India, in line with the basic suppositions of inequality that underlie Hindu thought, castes are hierarchically ranked in accord with considerations of ritual purity. The groups of people practising more polluting occupations and having less desirable styles of life are lower in the hierarchy; the others, higher. In all-India terms, groups of castes can be viewed as positioned according to the *varna* classification, with Brahmins, priests and teachers, at the top; Kshatriyas, warriors and administrators, second; Vaisyas, merchants, next; Sudras, farmers, next; and "untouchables" (Harijans), at the bottom.

Helpful as is the *varna* scheme for classificatory purposes, in general its usefulness breaks down when it is necessary to discuss a local ordering of castes. All over India, it is usually possible to find Brahmins at the top of a local hierarchy and various Harijan groups at the bottom. But, in between, the situation is far from easily described.

G.S. Ghurye has estimated that within any of the general linguistic regions of India there are approximately 2,000 distinguishable caste groups.[10] Whatever the accuracy of this estimate, it is usually common to find at least ten to fifteen castes residentially represented in a particular village and at least fifty that can be identified by local villagers. As a result, a strictly attributional ranking classification (such as the *varna* scheme) loses its specific applicability, and the interactions of castes in terms of their respective economic and political connections come to play a more important role in the actual positioning of the caste group.[11]

Attributes are important and the process of Sanskritization — the process whereby a lower caste is able, "in a generation or two, to rise to a higher position in the (caste) hierarchy by adopting vegetarianism and teetotalism, and by Sanskritizing its ritual and pantheon"[12] does help account for the changes in caste positions that often occur. The ranking of castes in villages and regions, however, is also related to a number of additional variables and never fits only a simple attributional rank ordering.

Early analyses often pictured the Indian village as nearly independent, as having within itself nearly everything it needed for subsistence. The village is, in fact, relatively self-sufficient. But to picture it as almost completely isolated is erroneous. Milton Singer writes summarily of the participants in the seminar on Indian village studies held at the University of Chicago, in 1953-54:

> They reported...that each village was linked to other villages in its region, and to towns and cities, by complex networks of social relations based on caste, kinship and marriage, trade and occupation, religious pilgrimage, and administration and political organization.[13]

In introducing the book of essays he edits, M.N. Srinivas says simply and with the same end in view: "The completely self-sufficient village republic is a myth; it was always a part of a wider entity."[14] The village in India is usually easily definable as a geographical entity and is, in general, clearly distinguishable in terms of its social system. At the same time, it is also tied into numerous more extensive networks.[15]

Some have assumed that such things as the "trip to town" and the introduction of more modern systems of transportation and communication lead inevitably to the destruction of caste and extended family kinds of considerations. Others, basing their perspectives on the fact that the characteristic forms of Indian social organization have always been adaptive in compartmentalizing differences, show that such forms remain important as organizing features of social life in almost all Indian settings.[16] These latter scholars see many changes taking place, of course, observing, for example, that caste units are becoming more and more politicized and that new channels of participation between the elites and the masses are emerging.[17] But they also observe, on the basis of careful investigations, that the characteristic features of Indian social organization persist along with the newer forms.

The debate concerning which perspective is the more "correct" will go on. Yet, the latter already appears by far the more generally acceptable. Finally, it is not possible to conceive of the rural and the urban as discontinuous with each other in Indian civilization.[18]

CASTE

Organization

Caste certainly does not play as important a role in the lives of the Chennanagar people as it does in the lives of India's villagers. But it is important here and it does provide a convenient grid according to which to view comparatively the social organization of Chennanagar. The caste identifications of the Chennanagar people, the numbers of households and people in each category, and the customary occupation or occupations of each caste are given in Table 4.1.[19]

Just as in India's villages, no Chennanagar person of an accountable age finds it difficult to give himself and his relatives a caste identification. In both places, the question of caste is a natural one. The situation in Chennanagar, however, is very different from that in rural areas. First, it is different in that here most of the caste identifications voluntarily given by the people refer to clusters of castes rather than specific castes. In a particular village area, the name Reddy, for example, if used, commonly refers to a specific subdivision of the general Reddy caste. In Chennanagar, this name is claimed by persons of widely different geographical and occupational backgrounds. Six of the Chennanagar Reddy families come originally from the

Table 4.1

CHENNANAGAR CASTES BY NUMBER OF HOUSEHOLDS, NUMBER OF
PERSONS, AND CUSTOMARY IDENTIFICATIONS

Caste[1]	Number of households	Number of persons	Customary identifications
Ambattan	1	3	Barbers
Balija[2]	1	6	Cultivators
Chettiar	21	86	Traders
Devangi[2]	4	16	Weavers
Golla[2]	5	21	Herders
Gounder	4	21	Cultivators
Harijan	21	99	Untouchables
Idaiyar	2	4	Herders
Kammalan	12	50	Artisans
Kolabar	2	14	Potters
Kshatriya	2	8	Warriors
Mudaliar	29	168	Traders, contractors
Muslims[3]	4	24	Shopkeepers, tailors
Nadar	18	95	Toddy-tappers
Naidu[2]	42	180	Cultivators
Nair[4]	5	25	Landowners, artisans
Naicker	137	712	Cultivators
Padmasalle[2]	7	36	Coarse cloth weavers
Pillai	20	90	Cultivators
Reddy[2]	9	43	Cultivators
Udaiyan	1	4	Cultivators
Vadarazu	13	66	Labourers, masons
Wannan	1	7	Washermen
Mixed Caste	15	72	—

[1] By alphabetical listing.

[2] An Andhra caste.

[3] The Muslims, of course, are not actually members of a Hindu caste. Yet they can often be treated as a caste group in many South Indian settings. In Chennanagar, they respond to the question of caste by identifying themselves as Muslims.

[4] A Kerala caste.

Rayalseema side of Andhra Pradesh; the other three, from the coastal areas. These sets of families are not members of the same endogamous group. Yet all nine families similarly identify themselves as Reddys, ignoring the differences that exist, except at times of marriage.

A similar situation exists for many of the other castes given in the

Table 4.1 listing. These groupings are similarly composed of endogamous castes that in their native rural settings have different rights and obligations though they are of the same general caste level. Naidu is a title of honour and has been used by such Telugu castes as the Balijas, Boyas, Gollas, and Kapus. Naicker is the Tamil equivalent of Naidu and has been returned by Pallis, Irulas, and Vedans, among others.[20] Though there are subdivisions of the Harijan classification in both Telugu and Tamil areas, all but two of the Chennanagar untouchable families identify themselves only as Harijans, clearly preferring it this way.

The label Kshatriya (like Vaisya) is difficult to apply anywhere in South India but is used in Chennanagar by two related families. The Ambattan, Balija, Devangi, Golla, Idaiyar, Kolabar, Nadar, Padmasale, and Wannan caste names listed in Table 4.1 are relatively caste specific. The others, given as volunteered by the people, are more general, assumed in Chennanagar by castes quite different from each other.

A second difference between the organization of castes in Chennanagar and in rural areas is that here there is almost no residential segregation by caste. With as many Naicker households as there are, as many as four such households are contiguous with each other in places. Eight Harijan households are located together along Kalaignar Karunanidhi Street. Otherwise, the huts of the different castes are thoroughly interspersed. The people moved into Chennanagar and laid claim to the plots available without regard for their respective caste backgrounds.

A third difference has to do with occupational affiliations. At least ideal-typically — but even now, to a certain extent, in reality — castes in rural areas are hereditarily associated with particular occupations. In Chennanagar, most of the Padmasales are still weavers, most of the shops are owned by Chettiars, the Kolabars are engaged as potters and two of the Kammalan families gain their incomes through their hereditary work as artisans — one of them is headed by a goldsmith, the other by a carpenter. Otherwise, there is no correlation between caste and traditional occupation in Chennanagar. The occupations of the Naickers range from coolie to milk vendor and *beedi* maker, those of the Mudaliars from weaver to astrologer, and those of the Pillais from fruit seller to mason. A range of occupations is evident for almost all castes.

Fourth, and perhaps obviously by now, there is no correlation here between caste and such things as dress, manners, and styles of life.

Fifth, though eating meat and drinking alcohol are considered less favourably than vegetarianism and teetotalism, few people here practise careful dietary restrictions. All but three of the Chennanagar households serve mutton, fowl, and fish when they can afford to. About half of the Harijan families, the Muslims, and a sprinkling of others eat beef from time to time. The others never do. Such are general restrictions only, though, and they are the only kind observed. By and large, the people eat with whom they wish and the very specific dietary restrictions usually found in the villages cannot here be observed.

A sixth difference has to do with attitudes towards Brahmins. Here Brahminical authority carries very little weight. In part, this is due to the fact that there are no Brahmins in Chennanagar and the immediate setting and thus this group of people has little local relevance. It is also due to the kinds of influences the DMK and other groups have spearheaded in recent years. The Brahmins, early privileged as they were in religious authority and economic power, in the past were able to exercise a political influence in South India out of all proportion to their very small numbers.[21] They were also able to gain an early access to systems of western education and thus to find, early, jobs in the colonial administration.

The non-Brahmin movement, the movement for which the DMK is today the leading political organization, in turn, was not long in emerging. It was fuelled by feelings of jealousy and repression. Its negative objective was to prevent the control of the government by the Brahmins, its positive objective "to capture political power with a view to introduce statutory measures to minimize the Brahmin preponderance in public services and to restrict their entry into technical, professional and educational institutions."[22]

Such emphases have filtered to the lower socio-economic levels of the Madras population in recent years. And, certainly, they have filtered into Chennanagar. The political successes of the DMK have been spectacular and, based as these successes have been on the widespread mobilization of support, the teachings of the Dravidian movement have become well-known. Anti-Brahminism is more easily associated with some of the earlier periods of the Dravidian movement than it is with the DMK period. But some of the consequences of the earlier attacks against the Brahmins persist.

A final difference between the organization of caste in Chennanagar and in rural areas is that here there is almost no ranking of the castes according to ritual purity.[23] Most of the caste identifications given are general rather than specific. As a result, the differences in the ritual standing of the particular castes within the more general groupings are often as great as the differences among the groupings, making it relatively meaningless to compare the respective standings of the castes.

Other reasons for the minimal ranking by ritual purity, in Chenna-nagar, include the following. First, in the conditions of poverty in which the people find themselves, ritual purity is a matter of relatively little concern. It means far less to the people than does, for example, economic security. Second, there is little functional interdependence among the various castes in Chennanagar. Whereas in the villages rights and obligations can be correlated with specific caste positions, here there is almost no correlation between a person's style of life and his caste position. People fend for themselves in whatever ways they can and status by ascription is no guarantee of any kind of privilege. Third, Chennanagar contains such a variety of people—Tamils as well as Telugus and Malayalees, people with urban as well as rural backgrounds, and so on — that the consensus necessary for the people to evaluate collectively the differences that exist can hardly emerge. Fourth, due to the kinds of influences that today are most prominently represented among the teachings of the DMK, people in places like Chennanagar are far less concerned with ritual position than they once were. Finally, new as is this community, interaction patterns here are still not clear.

Thus, such important corollaries in the ranking process as degree of dominance and prestige of occupation have not yet become adequately described. But given the fact that most of the Chennanagar castes are of roughly similar socio-economic levels (a situation that makes inter-actional patterns as important as attributional patterns in determin-ing a caste's specific ritual rank), such corollaries must be adequately defined if a ranking system itself is to become clear.

Some Chennanagar Kammalans are of the Panch Brahma group of castes and legitimately wear the sacred thread that signifies their "twice born" status.[24] Eight people claim the status of Kshatriyas. Most of the Chettiars consider themselves Vaisyas. Ninety-nine persons are Harijans. With the rest (88 per cent) of the people belong-ing to the Sudra *varna*, it is not difficult to order the Chennanagar people according to the *varna* scheme. However, it is hardly meaningful to do so. The divisions thus possible are too general to be of much use. In addition, the higher caste claims of some of the people are very sarcastically viewed by most of the people. The distinctions between the Harijans and the others remain more clear than some of the other distinctions. But even here there is little evidence of the kind of discrimination that can be found in rural areas.

Summing up, the people of Chennanagar are aware of their own caste identifications and that of their fellows. But the organization of caste in Chennanagar is different, in many ways, from the organization of caste in more traditionally defined areas.

Persistence

However, in addition to being important in naming, caste considerations also remain important as organizing features of social life in Chennanagar. Most significantly, such considerations remain basically important at times of marriage, just as they still do in India as a whole.[25]

Specifically, Table 4.1 shows that only fifteen Chennanagar households (4 per cent) can be classified as mixed caste households, on the basis of what the people report. Now, the number of inter-caste marriages would be higher if all of the subdivisions of the general castes could be taken into account. It is also probably higher than the number of such marriages reported. But still, only fifteen were reported.

Moreover, on the basis of interviews with the people, it is clear that in talking of preferred marriage arrangements, by far the majority have preferred for themselves and prefer for their children, marriages within the particular caste units to which they belong. A Naidu-Balija married to a Naidu-Boya explained it saying: "When we are married, we were forced to leave our village. And since, we have had nothing to do with our people. Our own children don't really fit into any caste. It seemed the right thing to do when I married but if I knew then what I know now, I would not have done it." A woman of an inter-caste marriage said: "If people were not so careful in arranging their marriages, it would not have been so difficult for my husband and me, and for others like us. We have been rejected by our families."

There are signs of change in the established patterns of marriage, and a number of people would agree with the feelings expressed by a Mudaliar woman:

If I had a daughter now, I would rather give her to a rich man than to a Mudaliar. I was young when I was married and feared what my relatives would say if I asked for an inter-caste marriage. But now it makes no difference to me. My ancestors cared about sub-caste in arranging marriages. My parents began to think only of the general caste of the man I married. If I had a daughter ready for marriage now, I wouldn't think of caste at all.

In general, though, the preference for marriage arrangements within caste units continues. None of the Chennanagar people involved in inter-caste marriages are closely associated with the other members of their families. This makes it difficult for them in certain ways, for most people retain to the extent possible at least some affiliations with the social environments to which they originally belong (see Table 4.2), thus possibly gaining some economic and other advantages.
⌐ Inter-caste marriages tend to cut off individuals from their families. They also tend to make it difficult for parents to arrange suitable marriages for their children, as children of such unions tend to have very ambiguous identifications, especially where the parents include both a Harijan and a non-Harijan. In fact, whatever loosening up there might be in the arrangement of inter-caste marriages seems to be occurring almost exclusively at the Sudra level. Marriages across the more basic line between Harijans and non-Harijans are still, generally, quickly shunned.

Another indication of the continued importance of caste-like considerations in Chennanagar is that here the process of Sanskritiza-tion is still apparent. It is made unclear by the variety of influences

Table 4.2

FREQUENCY OF ASSOCIATION (BY PER CENT) BETWEEN CHENNANAGAR
PEOPLE WITH RELATIVES OUTSIDE NORTH MADRAS

Frequency of association	*Per cent*
About once a year	42.1
Two or three times a year	20.4
Four or more times a year	13.4
Never	19.1
Almost never	5.1

that impinge on Chennanagar, and is by no means unilinear. Yet dietary restrictions are often positively regarded by the people and those practises considered higher are adopted by families concerned with their status, if these families can afford the adoptions. For example, beef is commonly considered a food for Harijans and Muslims only, and even some of these people, influenced by the ideas of their context, have given up eating beef.

A number of the Chennanagar castes have laid claim, legitimately or not, to "twice-born" status, and are themselves convinced they deserve the status they claim. In short, caste labels are used in Chennanagar to identify general eating habits, etc., and persons, when considered in terms of attributes, are considered as members of groups. And such is the "stuff" in relation to which the processes of Sanskritization work.

A third factor is that many verbal stereotypes still follow caste lines rather closely. The following are some common proverbs: "No matter how clever an Idaiyan may be, he is still a little stupid." "Never believe it if a black man says he is a Brahmin or a red man that he is a Madiga." "A Wannan is more clever than an educated man." "If you want to kick a Madiga, you can speak to him and then kick him, but with a Mala, never speak to him, just kick." "A Paraiyan will never understand a joke until he has walked a mile."[26] The stereotyping in such proverbs is exaggerated, of course, but the proverbs point out some of the features of the learning context associated with caste.

Another indication of the continuing importance of caste in Chennanagar is the readiness of the people to speak of their own identifications and those of their fellows. The major distinctions — those between the Harijans and others, and those between the Brahmins and others — are the ones most readily recognized. But more specific identifications can also be easily elicited.

Finally, whether or not caste has become unimportant in Chennanagar, caste is still of underlying significance in the broader context — in political life, in general living, and in relation to its organizing role in the ecological patterns that occur in Madras. With reference to the role of caste in Tamilnadu's political life, the convention in Madras mayoral elections has been that a non-Brahmin Hindu, Brahmin, Muslim, Christian, and Harijan, in turn, be selected for office. The British evolved this system to guarantee the political representation of all of the major communities in the population. By now, however, at least in the eyes of the Chennanagar people, the meaning-fulness of the rotational representation by general community has broken down and castes rather than communities vie for the position of mayor.

This view, in turn, finds support in the following statement by the Harijan councillor for the Ward 21 area.

> In the corporation council, there is much caste feeling. A DMK Naicker will often get along better with a Congress Naicker than he will with a DMK Harijan. The Brahmins always feel they belong to the highest caste in the world and that they are superior to the rest of us. People today are not willing to express openly their feelings about caste because they have been told not to. But everyone knows the caste of those he associates with.

Political relations in Madras and Tamilnadu are not arbitrarily manipulated by any caste or collection of castes but such relations are still channelled by the influences of caste. Writing of Kamaraj Nadar, in relation to the "Tamilization" of local politics, Robert Hardgrave points out that "... [he] forced the Congress to face a rather rustic reality, that caste is very much a part of politics in India."[27]

In reference to the persisting role of caste in general, Joan P. Mencher notes that caste is becoming something more than it was but that the system remains operative in all Indian social settings. She writes:

> In urban areas in the South informal caste groupings help their fellows at least in providing a social forum, and on occasion, in more matters. If a member of the caste has arisen in importance either in government or in private business, he will make use of these informal relationships within his caste group in selecting recipients for favours (assuming that his close relations are not in the bidding) or in deciding whom to hire.[28]

Meanwhile, in that castes as units are identified as belonging to "backward classes," "scheduled castes" and so forth—classifications defined by the government as eligible to receive special assistance and guarantees — the meaningfulness of caste as an organizational label is encouraged in the general area.

Finally, in reference to the ecological structure of Madras, Jay

Weinstein shows how traditional features of Indian social life persist here, and thus how this city's ecological structure can hardly be adequately understood in terms of the conventional structural models used in the West.[29]

Perspectives

The Chennanagar context is entirely different from the rural context in which caste retains more of its identifying, traditional features. Furthermore, the economic, political, ideological, and social factors that are effecting changes in the organization of social life in rural areas are also effecting changes in Chennanagar. The Indian government with its secular emphases has often labelled caste a carry-over from the past and has often assumed it has little significance for the present. Discrimination on the basis of caste has been legally prohibited, and untouchability has been outlawed. Many officials in modern India have been drawn from among the lower castes and all of the people must interact with such officials should they desire the services they offer.

The messages of Mahatma Gandhi, Jawaharlal Nehru, and others come into places like Chennanagar and modify local understandings. Education spurs changes. Taught of some of the worst aspects of living in filth, many of the poor in places like Chennanagar have improved their standards of cleanliness. In democratic India, votes are needed for election to office and politicians are well aware of the need to maintain effective relations with different groups of people no matter what their social standing. "Outside" notions of the basic equality of all people have filtered into local settings and have caused people who have lived under the inequalities of the ascriptive system of caste to question its premises.

Public facilities have necessitated adaptations. Persons who travel together in buses and trains, or sit together in hotels or other places, are often strangers to each other. As a result, their interactions are naturally often guided by considerations other than caste. Some people take precautions. For example, one Chennanagar person who eats in places in which he does not know who prepares the food and under what conditions of purity, explains: "In such places, I close my eyes from time to time and say 'Rama or Krishna'." But even such precautions are not practised by most of the people. The situation does not encourage it, as many changes have occurred.

Nevertheless, as we have seen, caste does remain important in

Chennanagar. How then might we conceptualize the situation as it now is?

In his article, "Multiple Reference in India's Caste System," McKim Marriott explains that systems of ranking in metropolitan and rural settings must be distinguished. He sees

(1) the metropolitan ranking system as (a) an open, universalistic, and almost infinitely expansible system; (b) its typical units are individuals or small groups whose backgrounds are somewhat ambiguous; and (c) their comparative ranks are measured attributionally, i.e., highly visible behavioural modes are evaluated against a general urban scale of values. He contrasts with this (2) the rural ranking system, which, (a) is a closed system, comprising fixed sets of carefully identified castes, groups, and individuals; (b) their ranks are measured interactionally through daily confrontations that manifest ritual standing in terms of a purity-pollution scale; and (c) the units in the ritual stratification scheme of castes are corporate and, in innumerable ritual interactions, individuals are assumed to duplicate the performance of all other members of their caste.[30]

In many ways, the Marriott conceptualization of the metropolitan ranking system is applicable to an understanding of the problem of caste ranking in Chennanagar. The system here is indeed open and infinitely complex. Chennanagar is influenced by the wider urban milieu in every sense. The local community does delimit certain patterns of social life. But the local community is in no way "closed" in the sense that is necessary for a "rural ranking system" to emerge.

Applicable as it is, though, the Marriott analysis of differences between metropolitan and rural ranking systems is not enough, for it disallows a conceptualization of caste in the metropolitan context. Necessary as a correlate, then, is something referring to the local influence of caste. Again, caste persists in the local and in the more general contexts of Chennanagar.

Dennis Dalton has shown that in certain Indian settings caste is losing its hierarchical character but is still important as a "horizontal" system of classification.[31] In this he adds to the Marriott conceptualization what is needed to view the workings of caste in Chennanagar.

In the Madras with which the Chennanagar people are familiar, Brahmins might be placed at the top of a three-fold ritual ordering of castes, Harijans at the bottom. At an intermediate position on such a purity-pollution scale—clustered together in more general units than they were in the rural areas from which they first came but, anyway, more "horizontally" than hierarchically arranged—would come the other castes. The authority of the Brahmins has been attacked in Tamilnadu, but they retain much of the prestige that has long been associated with their caste. In fact, the volume and tone of the opposition to their position reveals their continuing privileges. The Harijans, meanwhile, though their position is much improved in modern India, are still generally regarded as below the rest of the castes.

FAMILY

Preferences

A few of the Chennanagar people prefer nuclear family to joint family living. They say that to live together with elders or other married relatives leads to quarrels, questions of who should do what work, who should have the most authority and so forth. And some of these people have wild stories of family fights to back their claims.

But most of the Chennanagar people have a distinct preference for joint family living. They explain this as follows, to cite the explanations given by three different adults:

If parents and children live together, with their wives, it is easier to run a business. It is then possible to work together and make more profit, and this adds up, bringing more prestige to the family.

Although there will be quarrels between the sons' wives and the mother-in-law, the head of a family that stays together can settle these. How good it would be to live near my father and mother when they get sick or to the age when they will die! When people live very close together, they can comfort each other and care for each other.

There is nobody around in times of emergency when children go off and live by themselves. Suppose a person loses his job. Who will support him and his family if he cannot get another job quickly?

The Chennanagar people live in a new community. Their conditions of poverty, economic insecurity, and relative disassociation from the more established patterns of life in the places from which they originate make them interested in the stabilities joint and extended family living can provide. They know of the ways in which kinship networks more extensive than those involved in common nuclear family living can provide a certain "insurance" to family members in times of economic hardship. And they know of the ways in which such family living can enable more extensive social and political associations, associations that have proven useful in many Indian settings, and their own (at least in the past), in finding capital investment capabilities, emotional encouragements, recreational diversities, care for children, care for the mentally and physically disadvantaged and so on.[32]

Few of the Chennanagar people came originally from villages. Yet even in Washermenpet, the much more established slum area from which sixty-four per cent of them came, the people agree they lived in much closer relationships than they now do with other members of their kinship networks.

Whatever the advantages many see and remember, however, the majority of the Chennanagar people feel that joint and extended family living is breaking down. The most general explanation they give for this can be phrased as it was by a young head of a nuclear household: "With the situation as it is, each person must do the best that he can for himself. It was my decision to move to Chennanagar with my wife and children — nobody forced me. Now it is all I can do to make a living for us alone."

In short, the most general explanation given for the decline in joint and extended family living has to do with economic factors. And these are very powerful. As we shall see (in Chapter Five, particularly), the parameters of the job market in Madras, for the poor, necessitate their doing the best they can under very difficult conditions. And as well as many of them do, it is also true, in general, that it is difficult for an individual from the poorer classes in the city to find regular employment and job security. Then too, the kinds of traditional kinship linkages that emerged and served so well in guaranteeing economic opportunities in the context of India's "little communities"[33] cannot institutionally function efficiently in modern Madras, open-ended and rapidly changing as is this context in terms of possible social, political, and economic associations. Certainly the Chennanagar people are insightful in explaining some of the changes occurring in relation to economic considerations.

They also use additional explanations, however, including explanations that have to do with the kinds of factors that underlie the peculiarities of caste in Chennanagar, the increased geographic and occupational mobility of the people, and the general feeling that children now do not grow up with the same respect for their elders that they once did.

Most Chennanagar parents with salaried jobs work away from home. Many adults look for jobs on a day-to-day basis, leaving home early everyday to find work. During the day it is not uncommon for the youngest children in a family to be left in the care of children only a little older than they are. Children are often left much to themselves and early learn to care for themselves. Given the conditions under which they live, they learn the facts of life at an early age. They also learn very early to make do with very little and to cope with many of the insecurities of their environment.

Parents and children in Chennanagar enjoy many things together and help each other when they can. Many of them go on pilgrimages together. Many of the local quarrels take place in relation to family loyalties. Parents do their best to help their children. They understand and themselves participate readily in such things as attempts to make good marriages for children of marriageable age, attempts to help children get promotions in their jobs, attempts to help them meet "important" people, and attempts to show off their children.

But try as they do for the sake of their children and though family members often do their best to help each other out, Chennanagar parents are handicapped in that they really cannot provide their children with much economic or social stability. At the same time, children growing up in Chennanagar have few formal advantages. Some of the young people of Chennanagar who have gone away to find jobs in other places send their Chennanagar relatives five or ten rupees from time to time. Few can afford to send more. Others send back nothing and some break all communication with their relatives.

Chennanagar houses are small. Locally, there are few economic advantages. The children grow up in a relatively undisciplined way. Given such things, it is not difficult to understand some of the explanations other than the economic that are given in Chennanagar for the breakdown seen in joint and extended family living.

Organization

In fact, by far the majority of the people in Chennanagar live in some form of the nuclear family. Pauline Kolenda has defined thirteen family types for purposes of comparison.[34] Using her definitions, the eleven types found in Chennanagar are: (*i*) the single-person household; (*ii*) the sub-nuclear family, a fragment of a formerly complete nuclear family; (*iii*) the supplemented sub-nuclear family, a sub-nuclear family plus some unmarried, widowed, or divorced relative(s), not part of the former nuclear family; (*iv*) the nuclear family consisting of parents and their unmarried children; (*v*) the supplemented nuclear family, a nuclear family plus some unmarried, widowed or divorced relative; (*vi*) the lineal joint family, parents with their unmarried children, plus a married son with his wife and unmarried children; (*vii*) the supplemented lineal joint family, a lineal joint family plus some unmarried, widowed, or divorced relative who is not a part of either of the component nuclear families; (*viii*) the collateral joint family, two or more married brothers, their wives, and unmarried children; (*ix*) the supplemented collateral joint family; (*x*) the polygynous, and (*xi*) the kinds of households that cannot be categorized in the types identified. Table 4.3 gives the distribution of family types in Chennanagar, according to Kolenda's typology.

Table 4.3

DISTRIBUTION OF FAMILY TYPES IN CHENNANAGAR

Family type	Households		Number of persons
	Number	Per cent	
Single-person household	12	3.2	2
Sub-nuclear family	26	6.9	66
Supplemented sub-nuclear family	9	2.4	39
Nuclear family	172	45.7	791
Supplemented nuclear family	75	20.0	368
Lineal joint family	48	12.8	327
Supplemented lineal joint family	4	1.1	26
Collateral joint family	9	2.4	75
Supplemented collateral joint family	11	2.9	101
Polygynous	8	2.1	40
Other	2	0.6	5

Table 4.3 shows (*i*) that 19 per cent of the households, housing 29 per cent of the people, are joint family units; (*ii*) that 66 per cent of the households, housing 63 per cent of the people, are nuclear and supplemented nuclear family units; and (*iii*) that the remainder of the people living in polygynous, sub-nuclear, and other types of family units. The percentages living in joint family units are lower than they have

been found to be in other places for which information is available. Yet, they are not excessively low, and in that a number of the supplemented nuclear family units might be listed as "extended families" it might be tempting to believe the structure of joint and extended family living in Chennanagar persists in a relatively unchanged way.

But this would be erroneous. First, despite the degree of association between the Chennanagar people and their relatives (and there is a good deal of this, as we have seen) and in other places (see Table 4.2), the association here is tenuous. It involves the selection of marriage partners. But it involves very little in the way of regular monetary exchange, the carefully defined exchange of goods and services, and the participation in an integrated pattern of life. Moreover, the joint and extended family living that does occur is more a matter of simple necessity than a matter of institutional form backed by common possessions, household engagements in a single industry or occupation, and other customary identifications. Whatever the preferences for older patterns of family living, the general pattern in Chennanagar is, thus, nuclear.

A Perspective

Raymond Firth has explained some of the changes likely to occur in an industrial setting as follows:

What the development towards an industrial society probably does is to break down the formal structure of kin groups,except perhaps that of the elementary family, which is most resistant. The lineage, the extended family, the large cooperative cognatic kin unit is likely not to survive as its members disperse into industrial employment and their traditional resources and authority structures lose meaning. But personal kin ties tend to be retained on a selective basis. Indeed, they may be even strengthened if the physical isolation of the elementary family is promoted by industrial, urban, conditions.[35]

Such a summary fits in the understanding of the family life that is now occurring more frequently among the Chennanagar people. Nuclear family living remains pervasive here while more extensive kin networks have broken down considerably.At the same time, though, an oiientation to a kind of living that allows for, and in certain ways encourages, more extensive family associations is evident. Given such an allowance and encouragement and the preference of many of the Chennanagar people for family living patterns more extensive than those involved in the nuclear family context, it is entirely reasonable to picture these people as being in a position to utilize selectively the kinds of associations their family networks enable whenever possible, and many of them do.

COMMUNITY

Following R. Warren, a community can be considered as "...that combination of social units and systems which perform the major social functions having locality relevance."[36] The latter involve production-distribution-consumption, socialization, social control, social participation, and mutual support.[37]

In what ways is Chennanagar a community — that is, in what ways do social units and systems here perform the major social functions having locality relevance — and in what ways is it not?

Already we know, of course, that the social life of Chennanagar is tied into the social life of Madras, Tamilnadu, and India in numerous ways. Just as in any other metropolitan or great traditional societal setting, we have been compelled to view local life in terms of the "vertical" networks linking it with more widely operating systems. Specifically, we know, for example, that the Chennanagar people use the transportational systems, communications facilities, police agencies, bazaars, pilgrimage centres, temples, schools, cinemas, and utilities available in their environments. We know also that their occupations and incomes, political power and usefulness, claims and offerings are not understandable in local terms alone. And we shall learn more of such dimensions of local life in the various chapters that follow. On the one hand, Chennanagar's social groupings do not thoroughly delimit social life in any area.

On the other, Chennanagar is increasingly becoming a community in its own right. The following points anticipate some of the understandings we shall later develop and summarize some of those we already have.

(i) Certain religious activities are locally performed and attended almost exclusively by the local people.

(ii) Chennanagar's people are united into a number of viable political groupings that administer a variety of activities while at the same time linking, through their leadership, the Chennanagar people into wider political networks.

(*iii*) At least in their earlier years, most of the children of this *nagar* spend the vast majority of their time here, locally learning how others in their setting "view their worlds" and relate themselves accordingly.

(*iv*) The Chennanagar people know who lives in this *nagar* and they know who comes in as an "outsider."

(*v*) They invite prominent "outsiders" to Chennanagar in relation to their own group affiliations and they pay these "outsiders" in ways that have to do with their abilities to provide collective support (in voting, for example) or collectively gained financial reimbursements.

(*vi*) In relation to their local political associations, they have the power to curtail the independent activities of some of their *nagar* fellows, and they exercise this power.

(*vii*) Together they help decide where public latrines are to be constructed and together they often complain of how these smell and how the smell might be alleviated.

(*viii*) Together, in a number of groupings, they seek added facilities for their *nagar* — for example, a school, a new temple, and street lighting.

(*ix*) Together they have acknowledged the leadership of certain local people and certain people in their context who are in a position to help them.

The move to occupy the Chennanagar land demanded that a collective action occur, and it did. Living in their conditions of scarcity has necessitated a local understanding of what can and what cannot be done, and this understanding is constantly emerging. The geographic outlines of this community, as easily distinguishable as they are, make it meaningful for the Chennanagar people to help each other out in things like extinguishing a hut fire, refereeing a fight, and organizing an activity.

The social patterns of Chennanagar are obviously much different from those that describe the social life of an Indian village. But, in terms of all of the functions that do play a major role in the definition of a community, various local groupings filter in, channel out, or locally help define at least some of the ways in which the Chennanagar people relate themselves to the elements of their surroundings and locally behave. Chennanagar is indeed a sociological community.

CONCLUSION

Is the social life of Chennanagar organized? Our evidence shows that caste and family patterns do not work here in anything closely resembling the ways in which they work in rural Indian settings. Yet it also shows that to the extent caste and family patterns can persist in a cosmopolitan urban setting — a setting marked by numerous economic and other shortages — they do. Clearly, certain of the "strengths" implicit in the time-tested structures of caste and family in India help organize the social life of the Chennanagar people.

At the same time, the Chennanagar people themselves are today building a community of a kind that enables them feelings of community consciousness and responsibility while simultaneously allowing them to get certain things done.

REFERENCES

[1] Examples of some of the better village studies are the following: S.C. Dube, *Indian Village*, Routledge and Kegan Paul, London, 1955; T.S. Epstein, *Economic Development and Social Change in South India*, Manchester University Press, Manchester, 1962; M.N. Srinivas, *Religion and Society Among the Coorgs of South India, op. cit.;* and Andre Beteille, *Caste, Class, and Power*, University of California Press, Berkeley, 1965. See also McKim Marriot (ed.), *Village India*, University of Chicago Press, Chicago, 1955, and M.N. Srinivas (ed.), *India's Villages*, Asia Publishing House, New York, 1960.

[2] J. Adams and Uwe J. Woltemade, "Village Economy in Traditional India: A Simplified Model," in *Human Organization*, 29 (Spring), 1970.

[3] See Harold A. Gould, "Time Dimension and Structural Change in an Indian Kinship System: A Problem of Conceptual Refinement," in Milton Singer and Bernard S. Cohn (eds.), *Structure and Change in Indian Society*, Aldine Publishing Company, Chicago, 1968; Pauline M. Kolenda, "What Changes are Occurring in the Structure of the Indian Joint Family?" a paper presented at the Inter-disciplinary Conference on Processes of Change in Contemporary Asian Societies, University of Illinois, Champaign-Urbana, 5-7 November 1970; Pauline M. Kolenda, "Family Structure in Village Lonikand, India: 1819, 1958 and 1967," in *Contributions to Indian Sociology*, IV, December 1970; and G.N. Ramu, "Family and Kinship in Urban South India," unpublished Ph.D. dissertation, University of Illinois, Champaign-Urbana, 1972.

[4] I will use "caste" throughout the text to refer to what is commonly labelled the *jati* in social-anthropological writings on Indian social organization.

[5] M.N. Srinivas, *Caste in Modern India and Other Essays*, Asia Publishing House, Madras, 1962, p. 30. See also the rest of the Srinivas book just cited, and another of his books, *Social Change in Modern India*, University of California Press, Berkeley, 1966, for comparative material and discussion on the definition of caste in India.

[6] Iravati Karve, *Kinship Organization in India*, Asia Publishing House, Bombay, 1965, p. 5.

[7] Residential segregation by caste is charted in many of the village studies published by the Government of India in relation to Census period investigations. For further information, see some of the village studies cited above and Paul G. Hiebert, *Konduru: Structure and Integration in a South Indian Village*, University of Minnesota Press, Minneapolis, 1971, pp. 50-53; and Paul Wiebe, "Small Town in Modern Indian," unpublished Ph. D. dissertation, Univesity of Kansas, Lawrence, 1969.

[8] M.N. Srinivas, *Caste in Modern India and Other Essays, op. cit.*, pp. 70-76, 148.

[9] M.N. Srinivas, *Religion and Society Among the Coorgs of South India, op. cit.*, p. 26. Taya Zinkin (*Caste Today*, Oxford University Press, London, 1962) says the moral code of a caste covers every aspect of life, "...not just how one prays, or whether one blasphemes, but how one cooks, when one works, to whom one

talks, even how one dresses." This is an over-simplification, but it allows an understanding of the extensiveness of caste concerns.

[10] G.S. Ghurye, *Caste and Class in India*, Popular Book Depot, 1957, p. 27.

[11] See M. Marriott, "Interactional and Attributional Theories of Caste Ranking," in *Man in India*, 39, and Paul Hiebert, *Konduru: Structure and Integration in a South Indian Village, op. cit.*, pp. 54-80.

[12] M.N. Srinivas, *Religion and Society Among the Coorgs of South India, op. cit.*, p. 30. On the process of and material concerning Sanskritization, see also Milton Singer, "The Social Organization of Indian Civilization," *Diogenes*, 45, April 1964.

[13] Milton Singer, *ibid.*, p. 96.

[14] M.N. Srinivas (ed.), *India's Villages, op. cit.*, p. 11.

[15] Paul G. Hiebert, *Konduru: Structure and Integration in a South Indian Village, op. cit.*

[16] See Dennis Dalton, "The Gandhian View of Caste and Caste after Gandhi," in Philip Mason (ed.), *India and Ceylon: Unity and Diversity*, Oxford University Press, London, 1967; Harold A. Gould, "The Adaptive Functions of Caste in Contemporary Indian Society," in *Asian Survey*, III, September 1963; K. Ishwaran (ed.), *Change and Continuity in India's Villages*, Columbia University Press, New York, 1970; Ramakrishna Mukerjee, *The Sociologist and Social Change in India Today*, Prentice Hall, New Delhi, 1965; G.N. Ramu and Paul D. Wiebe, "Profiles of Rural Politics in Mysore," in *Eastern Anthropologist*, XXIII, May-August 1970.

[17] See J.R. Gusfield, "Political Community and Group Interests in Modern India," in *Pacific Affairs*, 38, 1965; Lloyd I. Rudolf and Susanne H. Rudolf, *The Modernity of Tradition: Political Development in India*, University of Chicago Press, Chicago, 1967.

[18] See Owen M. Lynch, "Rural Cities in India: Continuities and Discontinuities," in Philip Mason (ed.), *India and Ceylon: Unity and Diversity, op. cit.*; K.V. Ramana, "Caste and Society in an Andhra Town," unpublished Ph.D. dissertation, University of Illionois, Champaign-Urbana, 1970; Jay Weinstein, "The Factorial Ecology of Madras," unpublished Ph.D. dissertation, University of Illinois, Champaign-Urbana, 1972.

[19] Edgar Thurston's seven volume *Castes and Tribes of Southern India*, Government Press, Madras, 1909, is the best general descriptive account of the characteristics, mythologies, and backgrounds of many of the castes referred to here. Other such accounts can be found in the various gazetteers available: for example, in John C. Boswell, *Manual of the Nellore District*, Government Press, Madras, 1873, and in B. Lewis Rice, *Mysore: A Gazetteer Compiled for Government*, Archibald Constable and Company, Westminister, 1897.

[20] Edgar Thurston, *ibid.*, p. 139.

[21] Chapter Six will deal with the story of the DMK in Madras. On the position of the Brahmins in the South, see Robert L. Hardgrave, "Religion, Politics and the DMK," in D. Smith (ed.), *South Asian Politics and Religion*, Princeton University Press, 1966, and S.N. Balasundaram, "The Dravidian (Non-Brahmin) Movement in Madras," in Iqbal Narain (ed.), *State Politics in India*, Meenakshi Prakashan, Meerut, 1967.

[22] S.N. Balasundaram, *ibid.*, p. 168.

[23] We tried to determine rank (i) by determining which groups would take food and water from which other groups and (ii) by asking informants from different castes to arrange cards with the names of the different Chennanagar castes on them, in ritual order. See Paul Hiebert, *Konduru: Structure and Integration in a South Indian Village, op. cit.,* pp. 54-80, on this. However, we were unsuccessful in both attempts. In the first, variations within castes were as great as the variations between castes. In the second, the people generally said, "Here we are all equal." Nevertheless, in the second attempt, the people generally put Brahmins at the top of a ritual ordering and Harijans at the bottom, when asked to deal with such general categories. But even this they did not do very voluntarily.

[24] On the meaning of the sacred thread and the Panch Brahma group of castes, see S.C. Dube, *Indian Village, op. cit.,* pp. 38-39.

[25] See G.N. Ramu, "Family and Kinship in Urban South India," unpublished Ph.D. dissertation, University of Illinois, Champaign-Urbana, 1972, and Paul D. Wiebe and G.N. Ramu, "Profiles of Rural Politics in Mysore," *op. cit.*

[26] The translations of some of the proverbs are simple. Others are less clear. The second one listed refers to the fact that higher caste people are generally lighter in complexion. The third refers to the ability of the Sakalis to sort things. Though they mix clothes together, the right articles get back to the right people. The educated man fumbles on this though he keeps a list. The fourth refers to the supposed relative cleverness of the Malas and Madigas. The Mals are supposed to be so clever they can talk a prospective beater out of a beating.

[27] Robert Hardgrave, *The Dravidian Movement,* Popular Prakashan, Bombay, 1965.

[28] Joan P. Mencher, "A Tamil Village: Changing Socio-Economic Structure in a Madras Village," in K. Ishwaran (ed.), *Change and Continuity in India's Villages, op. cit.,* p. 199.

[29] Jay Weinstein, "The Factoral Ecology of Madras," *op. cit.*

[30] McKim Marriot, "Multiple Reference in India's Caste System," in John Silverberg (ed.), *Social Mobility in the Caste System in India,* Mouton Publishers, London, 1968.

[31] Dennis Dalton, "The Gandhian View of Caste and Caste after Gandhi," *op. cit.,* p. 159.

[32] See G.N. Ramu, "Family and Kinship in Urban South India," *op. cit.,* and Milton Singer, "The Indian Joint Family in Modern Industry," in Milton Singer and Bernard Cohn (eds.), *Structure and Change in Indian Society,* Aldine Publishing Company, Chicago, 1968.

[33] Robert Redfield, *The Little Community: Viewpoints for the Study of a Human Whole,* University of Chicago Press, Chicago, 1955.

[34] Pauline Kolenda, "What Changes are Occcuring in the Structure of the Indian Joint Family?" Paper presented at the Inter-disciplinary Conference on Processes of Change in Contemporary Asian Societies, University of Illinois, Champaign-Urbana, November 1970.

[35] Milton Singer, "The Indian Joint Family in Modern Industry," *op. cit.,* p. 424.

[36] R.L. Warren, *The Community in America,* Rand McNally and Company, Chicago, 1963, p. 9.

[37] *Ibid.,* pp. 9-19.

Five

Economic Organization

DIMENSIONS OF POVERTY IN INDIA AND TAMILNADU

In their study of poverty in India, V.M. Dandekar and Nilakantha
Rath begin with a brief review of the situation as it was in 1960-61,
then review trends since that time.[1] Their table on the distribution of
population by per capita consumer expenditure, in 1960-61, is re-
produced here as Table 5.1.

Table 5.1

DISTRIBUTION OF INDIAN POPULATION BY PER CAPITA CONSUMER
EXPENDITURE IN 1960-61

Monthly per capita expenditure class (Rs)	Per cent of population (rural)	Per cent of population (urban)
0-8	6.38	2.15
8-11	11.95	5.49
11-13	9.88	7.19
13-15	9.82	6.86
15-18	13.79	10.71
18-21	11.44	11.40
21-24	9.03	9.68
24-28	7.72	11.03
28-34	7.66	9.34
34-43	5.93	9.61
43-55	3.12	7.04
55 and above	3.28	9.50

Source: Adapted from Table 1.1 in V.M. Dandekar and N. Rath, "Poverty
in India," *op. cit.*

Regarding the level of consumer expenditure that secures a diet adequate at least with respect to calories, Dandekar and Rath calculate that in 1960-61 about 50 per cent of the urban population and 40 per cent of the rural population lived below the desired minimum. At that time, given expenditure distributions for all commodities, about Rs 180 per capita per annum for rural households and Rs 270 per capita per annum for urban households were required to purchase the minimum quantity of food necessary to give the number of calories (determined by nutritional experts to be about 2,250 calories per capita per day) adequate for life under Indian environmental conditions.[2] With reference to the categories in Table 5.1, those in rural areas with monthly per capita expenditures in the lowest four categories, and in urban areas, in the categories from Rs 0-8 to Rs 18-21, plus about half the population in the category Rs 21-24, at that time lived on incomes inadequate even for basic food requirements.

Bad as the situation was in 1960-61, the profiles of poverty in India have now become even more severe. The per capita private consumer expenditure for Indians rose somewhat between 1960-61 and 1967-68, but these increases have not benefited all groups equally. Dandekar and Rath write:

The gains of development have remained largely confined to the upper middle and the richer sections constituting the top 40 per cent of the population. While the overall per capita consumption increased by 3.9 per cent in seven years, the consumption of the upper 40 per cent of the rural population increased by at least 4.4 per cent and that of the upper 40 per cent of the urban population by at least 4.8 per cent. . . . The middle, lower middle and poorer sections of the rural population showed much smaller increases in their per capita consumption and the per capita consumption of the poorest 5 per cent actually declined a little. The situation in urban areas appears even more serious. The per capita consumption of the lower middle and poorer sections constituting the bottom 40 per cent of the urban population declined and the consumption of the poorest 10 per cent declined by as much as between 15 to 20 per cent.[3]

Drawing conclusions from their study, Dandekar and Rath comment that persons unfamiliar with the patterns of life among, say the 40 per cent poorest rural population and the 50 per cent poorest urban population, wonder "how men at all subsist at these levels."[4]

Correlative figures show that in Tamilnadu a large proportion of the population also lives in poverty. In fact, with its large proportion of rural landless labourers and urban indigent peoples, Tamilnadu is one of the states with the highest incidence of people living in poverty conditions. In 1961-62, the percentage of rural and urban populations with an inadequate intake of calories came to 55 and 71 per cent respectively.[5] Meanwhile, National Sample Survey figures for 1968-69 show the average monthly per capita consumer expenditure to be Rs 33.67. The same figures show that 68 per cent of the rural population and 74 per cent of the urban population have monthly per capita expenditures below this level.[6] In that a monthly per capita expenditure between Rs 18-21 in rural areas and Rs 28-34 in urban areas was necessary to achieve a minimal adequate intake of calories even in 1960-61, it is clear that the situation remains severe and that the proportion of people in Tamilnadu living in conditions of "absolute poverty" remains about as it was.

POVERTY IN CHENNANAGAR

Many in Madras speak harshly about the ways in which slum people spend their money. For example, a former mayor of Madras, in an address before a seminar in 1971,[7] said among other things that slum dwellers commonly mask their incomes in order to fool welfare and distribution agencies concerning their needs; that they often own homes in better areas but prefer to rent them out, while they themselves live in slum conditions, in order to gain added income; that they are often immoral, maintaining wives or mistresses in several different slum areas, thus bringing their poverty on themselves; that political tendencies in Tamilnadu in recent years have so favoured the poor that it is now the middle classes rather than the slum dwellers who have a hard time making ends meet.

There is at least partial justification for each of the former mayor's charges. As almost anywhere else, a certain number of rascals, deviants, cheats, and "innovators" can be found in the slums of Madras. It is also true that squatting and other rights have often been given to the poor by politicians eager to gain their support.[8] Simultaneously, however, possible descriptions of slum life in Madras (as we shall see) show that such interpretations are very one-sided.

In fact, it is not easy to determine the precise incomes of people in a place like Chennanagar. Some, assuming that those who collect the figures are in one way or another connected with the government or other administrative or "help" agencies, and that the figures will will be used to their advantage or disadvantage, make unreliable estimates. Many tend to report only the incomes of those who are regularly employed, thus masking the total income of the household. Some can make only rough estimates themselves for their context of employment lacks consistency and their incomes vary widely from month to month. Recognizing these and related problems, we proceeded as carefully as we could, collecting figures on total household incomes. The Chennanagar per capita distribution of incomes is reported in Table 5.2.

Table 5.2

DISTRIBUTION OF CHENNANAGAR POPULATION BY PER CAPITA INCOME,
FIGURES COLLECTED IN MARCH 1970

Monthly per capita expenditure class (Rs)	Per cent of Chennanagar population
0-8	10.27
8-11	8.34
11-23	10.40
13-15	10.90
15-18	11.58
18-21	9.28
21-24	5.67
24-28	11.39
28-34	8.53
34-43	6.23
43-55	3.36
55 and above	4.05

The figures in Table 5.2 are not directly comparable with those given in the first section of this Chapter. Those given to sketch poverty in India and Tamilnadu give per capita consumer expenditure, those in Table 5.2 give per capita income. The figures in Table 5.1 are for 1960-61, some of the figures for Tamilnadu are for 1967-68, and those in Table 5.2 are for a month in 1970. Nevertheless, a rough comparison of the sets of figures identifies the very low standard of living in Chennanagar.[9] Whereas in urban India in 1960-61, only a little more than 2 per cent of the people were in the monthly per capita expenditure class, Rs 0-8, in Chennanagar, more than 10 per cent even today report incomes in this category. About 86 per cent of the people make less than the average per capita consumer expenditure (Rs 33.67) for the state. Using the Rs 28-34 figures considered necessary to secure the provisions for a minimum adequate diet, more than 80 per cent of the Chennanagar people are below the "absolute poverty" level.

On the other hand, nearly 15 per cent have monthly per capita incomes that fall into the top three income categories. Some of these could afford to live elsewhere. Others couldn't. But only for this very small minority would it be possible to say that they now willfully stay in such living conditions.

MAKING A LIVING

However, no matter how real poverty is in Chennanagar, and no matter how such poverty is interpreted by others, almost all the people make enough money to get by and very few rely on any more than minimal contributions from outsiders. Their ability to do so is part product of the jobs they can find, part product of their own ingenuity.

Principal Occupations

In occupational terms, the Chennanagar heads-of-households can be categorized as they are in Table 5.3.

Table 5.3

OCCUPATIONAL IDENTIFICATIONS OF CHENNANAGAR
HOUSEHOLD HEADS

Occupational category	Number	Per cent
Sales people	34	9
Skilled and semiskilled workers	52	14
Factory workers	15	4
Common labourers	172	46
Household industry workers	35	9
Shopkeepers	8	2
Miscellaneous	47	13
Unemployed	13	3
Totals	376	100

Table 5.3 shows that Chennanagar is not predominantly populated by persons engaged in any one traditional occupation, by factory workers or by household servants. It shows, rather, that they are engaged in a wide variety of occupations. A breakdown of the table's categories makes this even more clear.

Included in the "sales people" category are vegetable, fruit, and flower salesmen; milk vendors; cloth, blouse piece, and *lungi* (a cloth wrap-around for males) salesmen; and people who sell everything from popcorn, *idlis* (a steamed rice cake) and other food items to gunny bags, trinkets, cow dung patties, and *neem* tree twig toothbrushes. Those who sell things they first must purchase, make purchases at wholesale prices, then sell at a slight profit. The one person who sells kerosene makes a profit of 1 n.p. per litre. Others make similarly small profits, in general, sometimes more when they find they can. The household head who sells popcorn gets help from his wife and children in preparing and packaging small quantities, and sells these near Central Station. *Idlis* are made by women and sold locally by children at 5 n.p. apiece.

The income made in this way is the only income for one small household. In others, this possible income supplements the family's other income. Most of the Chennanagar sales people sell only one principal commodity: some sell for others who coordinate sales over a larger area, others work entirely on their own. But all except the two who work for regular handloom houses in the city sell things on a very small scale. Some carry their wares in baskets on their heads; others, if they have bicycles, in attached boxes. Such people advertise their wares vocally as they pass. Still others travel regularly to particular spots along larger streets and spread their wares for viewing. In the process, they add to the colour and confusion that characterizes so many of the city's bazaar areas.

In the "skilled and semi-skilled" category are sixteen masons and bricklayers; eight carpenters; five each dye-stampers and typesetters; three plumbers; two each painters, electricians, book-binders, printers, machinists, and turners; a welder, a goldsmith, and a metal worker. In village India, mason-bricklayers, goldsmiths, and metal workers are commonly found and generally associated with particular caste groups. In Chennanagar, the masons include Naickers, Vadarazus, Pillais, and Naidus by caste. The carpenters include Mudaliars, Naickers, Chettiars and there are only two persons for whom carpentry is a hereditary occupation. The only goldsmith is of the goldsmith caste. None of the household heads represented in the "skilled and semi-skilled" occupational listing practise their occupations at home. All work outside Chennanagar, finding work on their own or working under the supervision of contractors. One of the electricians, the metal worker, and the machinists have received some formal occupational training. The others have picked up on their own all they know.

In the "factory worker" category are seven household heads who work in a snuff factory, four who work in the Buckingham-Carnatic Mills, three who work in a peanut-oil mill, and one person 'who works at India Pistons Ltd. Four of these men are temporarily employed but hope for permanent employment; the rest are permanently employed and protected by union contracts.

Of the 172 "common labourer" household heads in Chennanagar, 131 are simply casual labourers who work when and where they can find it. Some pull carts in the streets and some load and unload ox-*bundies* (ox carts) or lorries. Others work as coolies on private construction jobs or in projects such as that organized by the DMK government to clean out the Cooum River. Of the balance, some are rail-road construction gangmen, sweepers employed by the Corporation of Madras, store helpers, firewood cutters, etc.

The "household industry" type employment category includes ten weavers, eight tailors, seven *beedi* makers, two cardboard box makers, a tanner, a potter, a lock maker, and a *dhobi* (washerman). The ten weavers merge into four joint families though they represent ten dwelling places. In turn, only one of these families weaves on its own. The others work for cloth contractors, getting paid at standard rates for the thread they dye or starch, and the cloth they weave. During the drier months of the year, a weaver family can expect to average about Rs 4 per adult per day in wages. During the most humid seasons, the income drops by as much as half because of the problem of breaking threads and the difficulty in handling thread. Whether or not a family works for wages, it must own its own spinners and handloom sets.

All of the major *beedi* factories in Madras — Kareem, Taj Mahal, Sait Clover, and Rustom —though they hire persons to work on their premises, also supply leaves, tobacco, and thread (the raw materials for making *beedis*) to persons in places like Chennanagar and pay these people to roll and label *beedis*. Labourers make Rs 2.50 for rolling 1,000 *beedis* and the more skilled can roll three to four thousand a day with some help from members of their families. Labourers also make Rs 0.15 for labelling 1,000 *beedis* and the more adept can label about 20,000 a day. One person recently started his own industry and now prepares, packages, and distributes *beedis* (Savitri Beedis) to sales people, commissioning them to sell for him. Like many of the others who do this in Madras, he is licensed by the Department of Industries and Commerce. Two other men work in the local area as distribution and collection agents for one of the larger factories. One, in addition, has hired some young people to label *beedis* under his supervision, paying them Rs 0.10 per thousand, keeping Rs 0.05 per thousand for himself.

Among the other household industries in Chennanagar are the cardboard jewelry box-making industry and the dye stamping (letter embossing) industry. Each investing about Rs 1,000 in the necessary paper cutting, "cornering," and other machines, the two families involved in box-making make plastic, heavy paper and cardboard boxes. An adult can make about 150 boxes a day, earning about Rs 12. In one of the households, two men and four boys working together make about 700 boxes a day. For hired help here, the household head pays Rs 5 a day per adult, Rs 1.25 for an older boy, Rs 0.75 for a young boy. Orders for boxes and sales are made through merchants along Anderson Street. The dye-stamping industry represents an investment of about Rs 2,500 (Rs 900 for one large machine, Rs 1,100 for two smaller machines, Rs 400 for dyes and dye blocks, plus miscellaneous moneys for recurring expenses such as powder, ink, etc.) and is organized by one household head, operated with the help of three young assistants. Orders for work are taken from merchants and others with expendable cash and involve such things as advertisements and marriage and festival announcements.

The potter, tinkers, weavers, and the *dhobi* all come from caste backgrounds that have these occupations as their hereditary occupations. The other household industries together involve people of a variety of different caste backgrounds.

Under the "miscellaneous" listing in Table 5.3 are forty-nine household heads representing many different occupations. One makes knives in a nearby *nagar;* another polishes stones; three are watchmen; six are peons; two each are bus conductors, taxi drivers, gardeners, and rickshaw pullers. The two Chennanagar astrologers sit in bazaar areas they are accustomed to and tell fortunes (one with the help of a parrot that picks cards) and read palms. Both willingly draw up horoscopes at special rates, and one has written articles for locally circulated Tamil periodicals on astrology. One Chennanagar person writes letters for illiterate customers. Another is a "special day" cook, hiring himself out as a cook for special occasions. Four men consider themselves brokers, one each for charcoal and lime, two for cereals. Whenever these men can, they arrange for purchases and sales, gaining commissions for themselves. Four Chennanagar household heads are clerks, two are retired constables, one is a public works department assistant, one drives his own ox-cart transporting goods in the city, one drives a lorry, and one contracts labour for construction projects.

Patterns of Economic Activity

The economic structure of most of rural India is agriculturally based and most village castes, with their specific occupational identifications, are tied into a division of labour related to agricultural activities. Ideal-typically, the *jajmani* system, with its specifications of interrelated rights and obligations between groups at different caste levels, tends to weld the entire village system together.[10] In fact, *jajmani* ties more clearly link together land owning and labouring groups, and service and upper caste groups, than some of the other groups that comprise the village system. The labourer and service groups in the *jajmani* network ideal-typically profit in terms of representation to important villagers and outsiders, "protection," and material rewards. The upper level groups (usually the patrons in the network) benefit in terms of labour guarantees, the performance of demeaning activities, and the like.

Fragments of the *jajmani* type of relationship can be found in many employment contexts in Madras. Relationships between the hired and the hirers, and sellers and buyers, often take on a patrimonial character and involve far more than simple monetary exchanges. Service personnel often carefully consider themselves the clients of those for whom they work, and expect, and often receive, special considerations because of their privileged relationship. In a good number of the occupations that can be linked with particular castes because of the hereditary occupations of these castes, a caste dominance of the occupation still holds and correct caste affiliation is almost a prerequisite to identification with such occupational groups.[11] For example, almost all of the sweepers in the city are of the untouchable Telugu castes, most of the *dhobis* of the washerman castes, and most of the barbers of the barber castes. In such groups, even though a money economy and other "modern" influences continue to make inroads on traditionally defined patron-client relationship systems, the same systems are still strongly operative. Where particular patrons can be identified, the patron families served by fathers are often also served by sons. And such patrons often give their clients gifts during special festivals or during special family ceremonies, and assistance during special times of need. In some sections of Madras — particularly in upper class residential areas where servants are still generally used — patron-client relationships of a traditional sort still link many families together. Finally, to the extent that caste continues to play a part in employment in many Madras occupational settings, fragments of the *jajmani* pattern of employment will also persist for the two are interrelated.

But, persistent as are fragments or even general features of the *jajmani* system, in Madras and in similar places it has not been possible for such a relationship network to persist in general. Such things as the surplus in labour, increasing mobility (in all its forms), a continuously diversifying occupational structure and an increasingly developing money economy have undermined its significance.

In Chennanagar, in fact, only one family — a weaver joint family— has a client relationship with certain patron families. And even for this family, the relationship is changing as it more and more comes to be defined formally rather than in terms of reciprocally understood obligations and privileges. None of the Chennanagar families are served by clients to whom they act as patrons.

In one sense, in turn, some of the employment and other securities of the people in Chennanagar and in the general Chennanagar context have been largely undermined. Yet, in another sense, and as we shall see below, a certain basic employment security persists for the people in both contexts.

Like the other major cities in India, Madras faces acute economic problems.[12] Problems of job security and suitable employment perplex many. The outlines of poverty being what they are, the economic situation obviously could be vastly improved. On the other hand, Madras, with its tremendous variety in peoples and needs, its industrial and commercial expansion, its combinations of the old and the new, and its labour intensive patterns of production and other economic activities, affords a setting in which there are almost endless numbers of ways in which to make at least a few rupees.

In short, the problem here has more to do with underemployment and unsuitable employment than with unemployment.[13]

The same is true for Chennanagar. Only thirteen persons here (see Table 5.3) claimed to be unemployed at the time of our survey. But at the same time, the degree of underemployment was extreme.

Many of the casual labourers in Chennanagar can work only when they themselves can find it, and so spend much of their time in search of work. Some of those who work on a contract basis are not contacted regularly. In fact, with the exception of the permanently employed factory workers, a few of the clerks, some of the peons, those who run their own shops and most of those engaged in household industries, all of the household heads work rather irregularly. With the diversity of occupations possible in Madras, almost all of those who wish to work can find some sort of employment. The only provisions are that the person must be willing to work in a job of low dignity, at low wages, and with almost no guarantee of continual or regular employment.

Turning away from the employment patterns of the Chennanagar people to another consideration, an understanding of the occupational identifications of the Chennanagar household heads alone does not adequately enable one to understand the ways in which the people make ends meet. First, though the greatest share is usually contributed by the household head, the total income of most households represents the work or the financial contributions of others as well. For most of the households engaged in household industries, the efforts of many individuals are involved. Even for the one potter family, for example, an elder child helps prepare the clay and the wife helps in the sale of the pots. About a third of the married women work irregularly as coolies, thus supplementing the incomes of their families, and more would work out of Chennanagar if more suitable jobs were available to them. Many unmarried boys work as coolies or earn extra money as they learn trades or attend school. In 19 per cent of households, at least one adult other than the household head also reports a regular income.

Second, there are many ways in addition to occupational employment in relation to which a little extra income can be made by a family. Two Chennanagar men have taken part in smuggling rice and alcohol into Madras, making a profit in the process.[14] One of the women who sweeps houses now sublets the right to sweep three houses to another woman, for Rs 2 a month, for she alone is unable to do all the work she has contracted. Several families own pigs, water buffaloes, and cattle, making a profit in the sale of animal by-products or in the use of the animals for draft purposes.

One man, a Central Station coolie for a number of years, because of an illness now allows another to work in his stead for a fee. Though the hiring and firing of Central Station coolies is formally defined, this man figures the right to his job is informally worth about Rs 1,000 and expects to gain this sum from the person he helps to become his successor. Like others in this employment context, the fact that he has a relatively permanent job is personally worth money to him, and others will pay him if he helps them gain his position, upon retiring, in turn also paying some money to the job supervisor for taking them on.

A third general consideration is that, in terms of job histories, an analysis of the patterns of employment of the Chennanagar household heads shows no consistent pattern of career development except in those involved in household industries. Almost all the household heads have simply taken jobs where they have been able to find them.

Attitudes Towards Work

There is no doubt that the Chennanagar people are willing to work. The luxury of being able to choose is not theirs for they must secure at least some income. Meanwhile, they hardly appear apathetic. The variety of their occupations speaks for the nature of the employment context; it also speaks for the ingenuity of the people, and their willingness to take on the kinds of jobs that are available.

However, the notion of hard work as an investment in occupational advancement and personal success is not well-developed here. One factory coolie put it like this: "We must work well and hard to keep our jobs. And we must be sure to respect the foreman and the managers. But we cannot get a promotion unless other people help us." Another labourer explained how he found his current job: "My father's brother works in the place where I work. When I was trying to find this job, my father gave his brother some money to give the supervisor so he would give me a job. The supervisor told my father's brother how much he wanted beforehand."

Again, it is not too difficult to find some sort of work. What is difficult is to make progress or find permanence in jobs without the payment of bribes, the help of influential outsiders, or such things as family and caste connections. By themselves, in short, the people have little influence and can hardly get things done. With help, on the other hand, they can accomplish many things. But this is the same problem they have in terms of their political context — and more will be said of this towards the end of the next chapter.

The Chennanagar people prefer clerical and governmental employment because of status and employment security, and many would like their children to find such employment some day. Considering the problems of their own employment context and encouraged by the Indian patterns of thought that identify manual occupations with lower social classes, few prefer manual over government or clerical jobs. But most of them cannot contest for the latter kinds of positions, for with their backgrounds, training, and associations, most of them are ineligible from the start. Most of them are more concerned with occupational security.

EXPENDITURES

It is generally true that the poorer the household, the greater the percentage of household income spent for essential items such as food and fuel.[15] This generalization holds true in Chennanagar. For the poorest here, there is little money for anything other than the basic necessities of life.

To represent patterns of expenditure in Chennanagar, the percentage figures for one month for eight Chennanagar households are given in Table 5.4.

The people in the households represented in Table 5.4 have relatively more stable and better incomes than the majority in Chennanagar. The average per capita expenditure here, for the thirty days in reference, comes to Rs 31.26.[16] But even for this set of households, about two-thirds of the total expenditure goes for food and fuel alone. Comparatively very little goes for medicines, education, religious observances, and clothing. The "other" category listings include payments for transportation, cinema charges, cigarettes and beedis, cooking utensils, household furnishings, water fees, rent, craft expenses, and the repayment of loans.

Other expenditures — expenditures that show up in part, but poorly, in budgeting lists because they are seasonal, not regularly planned for, and often involve loans — relate to marriages and funerals and other special ceremonies and occasions. Some of these involve proportionately large sums of money and many of them are extremely important.

Table 5.4

EXPENDITURE DISTRIBUTION BY MAJOR ITEMS FOR EIGHT CHENNANAGAR
HOUSEHOLDS FOR PERIOD 6 JUNE TO 4 JULY 1971

House-hold	Persons in house-hold	Total expen-diture for period (Rs)	Percentage expenditure distribution						
			Food	Fuel	Medi-cine	Edu-cation	Puja	Clo-thes	Other
1	9	351.95	55.66	3.42	5.58	3.21	1.69	3.26	27.18
2	7	251.51	55.33	5.10	0.40	2.88	1.74	3.54	31.01
3	9	209.98	66.40	7.74	1.31	1.73	1.09	3.68	19.15
4	6	154.51	71.46	2.76	3.88	0.96	2.76	5.19	12.99
5	5	178.01	63.48	2.39	1.28	1.87	0.86	3.51	26.61
6	6	199.59	62.36	4.79	1.05	0.36	5.03	1.67	24.74
7	7	162.33	62.89	4.61	0.00	7.68	0.00	1.49	23.33
8	7	242.61	63.66	2.84	4.10	0.58	2.28	3.60	22.97
Means			62.77	4.21	2.20	2.41	1.93	3.24	23.49

The conspicuous show of wealth here impresses easily. Furthermore, to the extent that bonds between families and other groups are strengthened and established during such occasions, investments in these facilitate the maintenance of meaningful relationship networks.

Actually, the range in expenditures for special events is wide, the amount spent depending on the wealth of the persons and their willingness to go into debt. The following descriptions of expenditures for earpiercing ceremonies and marriages illustrate some of the differences.

Some families spend almost no money on an ear-piercing ceremony, having the piercing done by a family member or relative at home. Others go to a pilgrimage centre, sometimes spending exorbitantly — one family reported spending Rs 1,000 in getting the ears of two children pierced in relation to a trip to Tirupathi. However, most have the piercing done in small, local ceremonies that serve as social as well as religious gatherings. The average expenditure at these can be represented by the following figures given for a 1970 ceremony for a Chennanagar child: Rs 5 for the services of the priest, Rs 2 for the services of an ear piercer (usually an area goldsmith), Rs 30 for the erection of a *pandal* (shelter) and some music, and Rs 50 for some food stuffs.

The one registered marriage[17] so far performed cost the couple the price of the license fee (Rs 30), the price of the garlands exchanged, and the price of the *thali* (a necklace symbol of marriage worn by the bride). The bridegroom's family spent about Rs 230 in providing a marriage feast in honour of the couple.

Temple marriages — more popular than registered marriages but less popular than traditionally conducted marriages — cost considerably more than registered marriages. They include payments for choultry rentals, travel expenses, the services of priests, and any meals that are served. In 1970, two temple marriages involving Chennanagar people took place at the Tiruvottiyur temple, each at a cost of about Rs 500. Another took place at Tirupathi for approximately Rs 200 more. Marriages in Madras cost proportionately less for no long distance travel expenses are involved.

One of the fancier, traditionally arranged and conducted marriages included the following expenses:[18] Rs 5 for the priest's initial examination of the couple's horoscopes; Rs 50 for travel expenses involved in an initial "inspection" visit by the bridegroom's party to the bride's house; Rs 480 for the bridegroom's party's gifts to the bride on the betrothal day; Rs 50 for the erection of the betrothal day *pandal;* Rs 100 for the betrothal day meal; Rs 80 for the erection of the wedding day *pandal;* Rs 60 for payment to musicians during the wedding period; Rs 300 for the bride's party's gifts to the couple at the wedding;[17] Rs 500 for the wedding day food; and Rs 200 for the bride's party's gift of a suit to the bridegroom.

Other expenses involved in the same marriage included the costs of the *thali,* travel expenses, the cost of the gold ring the brother of the bride received from the bridegroom at the wedding, other payments received by other participating priests, and so forth.

Very few of the Chennanagar people can afford fancy weddings of the kind described above, or elaborate ear-piercing and child-naming ceremonies. Obviously, considerable wealth, or at least very good credit is necessary to provide for such expenses, and few of the people have either.

SAVINGS AND INVESTMENTS

Very few of the Chennanagar people have any cash savings. Some of them have invested quite a sum of money in their household industries. Almost all have constructed the buildings in which they live and own the furnishings of these buildings. One family owns Rs 15 worth of Indian Government bonds on which it gets an interest return of about 6 per cent per annum. Fifteen or twenty families have post-office savings or bank deposits. Two or three older women wear small gold ornaments for their attractiveness and the investment they represent. Those who are permanently employed have the advantage of certain fringe benefits. But apart from such things, there is little long-term saving or investment in Chennanagar, and the only cash available is that which comes in relation to the work the people do and the little that some get in other ways.

Interestingly, the question of what a Chennanagar person would do if he suddenly obtained Rs 10,000 was answered for one person. Purchasing six tickets in the March 1970 state lotteries, S. Krishnan won a second prize worth this amount. With Rs 3,000 he paid off his debts and purchased new clothing for his family and jewelry for his wife. The balance he deposited in a savings account and now expects to buy three acres of land near his native place, Dindivanum. His father, who lives with Krishnan, will go to Dindivanum to till the soil; Krishnan will stay in Madras, holding on to the security of his permanent job in a local textile mill.

Krishnan claims he never knew he had so many friends before he acquired the money. But he has refused to spend foolishly, denying even his father-in-law a requested loan. Because of this, some people consider Krishnan to be miserly. One person, reflecting the feelings of many said: "This fellow acts no differently than he did before. Most of us would have spent some of the money in a celebration with our family and friends. We would have gone on a pilgrimage."

It would more likely than not be true, in village India, that at least some of the reward won by chance by an individual would be distributed among circles of friends and relatives. The sharing of wealth adds to an individual's social standing and helps guarantee assistance in times when he might need it. Finally, group affiliations for most people here are very strong, often resulting in a "levelling" off of an individual's personal gains.

The remark cited above and the earlier discussion of expenditure patterns indicate that at least some of the Chennanagar people would have engaged in a conspicuous sharing of their wealth if they had won money as Krishnan did. But in his own mind Krishnan acted wisely. For him, by far his most important responsibilities now have to do only with his immediate family. As more extensive social networks (such as those involving caste and the extended family) continue to lose some of their significance, it seems, in turn, that Krishnan's pattern of investment will become more and more common.

DEBTS AND FINANCIAL OBLIGATIONS

Most of the Chennanagar people in need of money are compelled to borrow from pawnbrokers along Wall Tax Road or in the Washermenpet area. In most cases, these shops are run by Marwadi businessmen who are commonly known to charge high rates of interest. However, with the impersonality of many of their employment situations, the people have little choice.

Rates of interest depend on the item pawned. If it is gold or silver, the interest rate is commonly 3 n.p. per rupee per month; if brass, 6 n.p.; for items like cycles, 10 n.p.; for clothes, 25 n.p. The item is evaluated by the broker who then gives a portion of its value, in cash, to the client. People with nothing to pawn and no securities are seldom given loans. But if they are, the rate of interest is about 10 per cent per month. Interest is levied on the sum borrowed, and collected at the time of the loan. Some of our Chennanagar informants estimated that 75 per cent of the people who pawn items are never in a position to reclaim them.

One popular way to raise money in many Madras slums is through "chit funds." According to this method, families requiring a considerable sum of money join together and once a month make contributions to a general pot. This goes on until each family has had a chance to use the monthly sum. The money is auctioned, first used by the family willing to pay the most for its use. The distributive process works in such a way that the person willing to wait until the end for his turn does not need to "purchase" the sum. Several "chit funds" were organized by groups of families when the Chennanagar houses were being built. Now, only one is locally organized.

Figures on debts in four slums in the northern part of Madras were collected by a private agency between August 1965 and January 1966.[20] These figures may not be especially accurate but they do give an indication of the level of indebtedness of many Madras slum dwellers. They range for the slums investigated — Cheriannagar, Desianagar, Asokanagar, and Pappanthoddam — from Rs 510.70 to Rs 209.71 per household, averaging Rs 333.06 per household. We collected no general information on indebtedness in Chennanagar, but we are confident the average debt per household here is less than it is in any of the slums mentioned above. Informally, we found only a few households with debts amounting to over Rs 300, most with debts lower than this and many households with no debts at all.

CONCLUSION

The people of Chennanagar are very poor, yet they do make ends meet in relation to the possibilities their environment provides and in relation to their own ingenious ways of finding work, gaining little bits of added income and helping each other out. The Chennanagar people need help (we shall have more to say about this in the concluding chapter) but they also obviously help themselves.

REFERENCES

[1] V.M. Dandekar and N. Rath, "Poverty in India," *op. cit.*

[2] V.M. Dandekar and N. Rath, *ibid.*, pp. 29-31.

[3] V.M. Dandekar and N. Rath, *ibid.*, p. 39. For comparative material on the deepening of poverty in India, see N.V. Sovani, *et al.*, *Poona A Resurvey:The Changing Patterns of Employment and Earnings*, Gokhale Institute of Politics and Economics, Poona, 1956; V.P. Pethe, *Demographic Profiles of an Urban Population*, Popular Prakashan, Bombay, 1964; and, for example, the Reserve Bank of India bulletin reported in the *Indian Express*, 16 April 1970.

[4] V.M. Dandekar and N. Rath *op. cit.*, p. 27.

[5] V.M. Dandekar and N. Rath, *ibid.*, p. 29.

[6] Reported in the *Indian Express*, 13 April 1970.

[7] The seminar was sponsored by the "77 Society" and held at the Madras Productivity Council offices, 24-26 June 1971. The theme of the seminar was, "Today's Children in Tomorrow's World."

[8] Cf. Ashish Bose, "The Process of Urbanization in India: Some Emerging Issues," in Richard G. Fox (ed.), *Urban India: Society, Space and Image*, Duke Universiry Press, 1970.

[9] Per capita private consumer expenditure rose 4.8 per cent between 1960-61 and 1968-69 in India, and income figures are usually a little higher than consumption figures (see V.M. Dandekar and N. Rath, *op. cit.*, pp. 25-35). Therefore, a comparison of the income figures for Chennanagar (Table 5.2) with the figures in Table 5.1 makes Chennanagar less poor than it actually is.

[10] For a general synthesis of some of the better materials on the *jajmani* system see Pauline M. Kolenda, "Towards a Model of the Hindu Jajmani system," *Human Organization*, XXII, 1963.

[11] For a historical view of the relations between castes and occupations in Madras, see H.V. Lanchester, *Town Planning in Madras*, Constable and Company, London, 1918.

[12] On this, see P.B. Desai, "Economy of Indian Cities," in *The Journal of Public Administration*, XIV, July-September 1968.

[13] For good material on patterns of employment in Tamilnadu, see the Finance Department of the Government of Tamilnadu publication, *Tamil Nadu: An Economic Appraisal*, 1971.

[14] General prohibition in Madras and Tamilnadu was lifted at the end of August 1971. Periodically, there have been rice shortages in Madras and Tamilnadu. Mysore, Andhra Pradesh, and Pondicherry, "wet" before Tamilnadu, were good sources for distilled liquor. Andhra Pradesh, commonly a rice surplus state during years of shortage and quota distributions in Tamilnadu, has often proved to be a good source for contraband rice. Small scale smugglers usually have very little trouble bringing commodities into the city.

The individuals in this trade in Chennanagar, either alone or with "helpers," have often hitched a train ride up along the coast (into Andhra Pradesh) in the morning, purchased what they needed, then returned with their contraband goods. At times they have been forced to hand over their goods to railway or police officials. But usually, when cornered, they have found a small "tip" to the official involved sufficient to allow passage.

[15] See V.M. Dandekar and N. Rath, *op. cit.*, pp. 26-27.

[16] The selection of households asked to keep records for a month was not random. It was based on our finding (in an earlier attempt to get expenditure distributions for a month) that the households with more stable and better incomes would be more willing and able, perhaps less embarrassed, to help us determine the patterns of expenditure.

[17] Registered marriages have never been very popular in India. They are still far from popular, in general. However, with such things as the increasing provision of insurance and other benefits for the widows of employees formerly employed in certain contexts, this type of marriage is becoming more common. Traditional marriages are legal, of course, but registered marriages usually result in more easily traceable records.

One Chennanagar informant explained the need for registered marriages as follows: "Suppose my wife is to claim guaranteed insurance benefits after I die and two or three women claim to be my wife. How will they distribute the money?" With a certain fragmentation of older social networks among the people, more legal definitions will continue to become more popular — perhaps in conjunction with more traditional forms.

[18] Among the Chennanagar people, as among many of the poorer in Madras, most of the wedding day expenses are borne by the bridegroom's party. Most of the expenses on the day of betrothal are borne by the bride's party.

[19] Gifts such as these are common but almost no formal dowries are now demanded by Chennanagar people. The demand is illegal in modern India, but this is not the explanation. Rather, the giving of dowries never has been especially popular among the people at the caste and class levels common in Chennanagar. Furthermore, the demand for the same has decreased in importance with emphases such as those the DMK encourages.

[20] The figures were collected by the Urban Rehabilitation project, Service Civil International and the Swallows, Tondiarpet, Madras-21. The mimeographed report of these figures is contained in a pamphlet entitled, "Social-Economic Survey: Family Case Study."

Six

Political Relations

THE CONTEXT

India is a democracy and democratic processes characterize the political life of the country at all levels of government. The interests of the villagers are represented to state governments through the multi-tiered, democratically defined *panchayati raj* system. Municipal corporations in the largest cities and municipal councils in the smaller cities represent the interests of urban populations to the state. States are represented to the central government through the parliamentary system defined by the Constitution of India.[1] Indigenous features of social organization, geography, language, and so forth, have yielded in India a unique blend of democracy. But for at least the last decade there has been little doubt that the electoral process is the only legitimate way in which to select leaders and that it is working.

S.N. Eisenstadt, viewing the consequences of modern political developments in India, observes that two closely interconnected aspects of change stand out:

> One is the expansion, together with the process of change, of the very scope of the field of social and symbolic participation of the different local groups and communities beyond the given locality or region....the second... has been the creation of a new centralized polity with a specifically modern ideology of political participation.[2]

F.G. Bailey, arguing similarly, points out that in democratic India, political activities in local "arenas" tie in with those in "elite arenas" more closely than ever before.[3] He shows how elections have placed more and more power into the hands of the common people. Simultaneously, he shows that as a result of the increasing contact between local and elite levels of politics, "middle arenas" of political organization are becoming increasingly well defined.

Chennanagar's political processes have been shaped by the kinds of developments to which Eisenstadt and Bailey refer. Elections are by now an integral part of local life and the people are becoming increasingly tied into political networks that extend beyond the borders of the *nagar*. Most clearly, perhaps, the developments that have occurred in Chennanagar can be understood in relation to the development of the Dravidian political movement. Before we look specifically at the political organization of Chennanagar, therefore, let us review the story of this movement in Tamilnadu.

TAMILNADU

Many integrating factors have been evident in the historical emergence of Indian civilization. The country finds unity in certain of its historic traditions. Hinduism and its related system of social organization are by and large coextensive with the boundaries of India. The country's networks of transportation and communication link together every corner of the country. The English language has served as a bridge language among the different linguistic regions and the country's administrative system extends even to the most remote villages.

Yet it is not by accident that the Indian Constitution centres a great deal of power in the federal government. This is because linguistic, cultural, and other differences have led to tensions in the past and have raised many questions concerning the nation's capacity to survive.[4] Demands for linguistic separatism led eventually to the reorganization of states in 1956, but the union was able to contain the centrifugal tendencies involved in the process. It also has been able to contain such disruptive tendencies as those involved in the reorganization of Bombay state in 1960, the periodic Telengana-Andhra disputes and the calls for more autonomy that have recently been voiced by the more militant groups in the north-east tribal regions of India. The union has also contained the demands for political independence that have periodically arisen in the Dravidian South.

Points of contention between the Aryan North and the Dravidian South in India have been reflected formally in Tamilnadu politics at least since the early years of this century. The Justice Party, founded in 1917 and formally called the South Indian Liberal Federation, sought to uplift the economic and social position of the non-Brahmins in the South. It claimed that the Aryans had locally introduced caste and related social distinctions in order to retain for themselves their positions of social superiority. Under E.V.Ramaswamy Naicker, the advocacy of a politically independent Dravidasthan began to gain strength, and in 1944 the DK (Dravida Kazagham), with this advocacy as its basic premise, grew out of the old Justice Party. In 1949, C.N. Annadurai in turn, seceded from the DK to form the DMK (Dravida Munnetra Kazagham). This party has since continued to work for what it considers to be the rights of the Dravidians.[5]

In general, the Dravidian movement has been a socio-religious revolt against Brahmins and Northerners, and Hinduism and Dravidian interpretations of South Indian history often lay stress on the conflicts between the immigrant Aryans and the native Dravidians rather than on processes of assimilation.[6]

No overt conflict occurs today between the North and the South, though manifestations of divergent interests are even now not uncommon. The 1937 attempts by leaders of the national liberation movement to introduce Hindi as a compulsory language in southern schools were violently repulsed, with the result that Hindi remained an optional subject for the time being. Similarly, the 1965-66 attempts by the central government to institute formally Hindi as the intra-Indian link language led to widespread demonstrations and the eventual rescindment of the attempt.

Both in 1937 and in the middle 1960's, the feeling widespread in the South was that the proponents of North Indian languages and ways were trying to suppress the languages and cultures of the South. Other occurrences point in the same direction and, in recent years, secessionist Dravidian leaders have continuously claimed that the South has been neglected in national development programmes and under-represented in national circles of power. Such leaders also have claimed that northern industrialists and commercialists consider the South an area for northern exploitation.

Over the years many of the negative emphases of the Dravidian movement have been softened. Anti-Hinduism is more easily identified with the DK than the DMK period. Anti-Brahmanism now refers less to the community of Brahmins than to the general feeling that some groups of people are by birth superior to others.[7] Meanwhile, continued interest by the country as a whole in the economic and other development of the South as well as the North has undermined some of the feelings of economic discrimination. Indeed, when a 1963 amendment to the Constitution made secessionist propaganda a punishable offense, even that official emphasis of the Dravidian movement was abandoned.[8]

The Dravidian movement, however, has emerged forcefully and the election successes of the DMK in recent years have been dramatic. The party emerged in 1962 as the leading opposition party to the Congress. It gained fifty of the state assembly's 206 seats and seven of the state's forty-one Lok Sabha seats. Then, in 1967, the DMK overwhelmed the Congress in both legislative body contests, taking 138 of the 234 seats in the Legislative Assembly and twenty-five out of thirty-nine seats in the Lok Sabha. The DMK's successes surprised many, for prior to the 1967 elections, no challenge to the dominance of the DMK and even this challenge left the Congress with a strong majority in the state's legislative assembly and a majority in Tamil-nadu's representation to the Lok Sabha. Furthermore, the Congress administration in the state prior to these elections was considered by many to be one of the best in India.[9]

Many reasons help explain the DMK rise to power. First, its success-ful emergence is related to the distinct regional awareness the move-ment fostered. Based as it was on the encouragement of indigenous ways and culture, the movement served the people ". . . as a vehicle for an expanding identity horizon" and gave them an increasing sense of belonging to a general Tamil community with its own interests and future.[10]

Second, the community thus formed came to include the masses as well as the non-Brahmin elites who had largely comprised the earlier Justice and DK parties. The leadership of the DMK continued to come from prosperous non-Brahmin groups like the Vellalas and the Mudaliars but the membership increasingly came to include persons from all social levels. With a declining anti-Brahminism, it also came to include some Brahmins and thus to divide the powerful opposition the DMK had earlier had from a united Brahmin community.

Third, the movement knew leaders who were able to focus into realizable directions the interests of the people and who, because of their capacities, were inspirational in mobilizing their supporters. For one thing, the movement's leaders, some of them in the course of time themselves coming from humble backgrounds, made a thorough attempt to identify the movement with the common people and to narrow the gap that often has separated leaders from followers in all parts of India.[11] For another, in the late C.N. Annadurai the movement knew a leader with whom the masses were able to identify.

Fourth, the DMK profited in the relationship that developed between itself and the cinema industry for this was a time when the popularity of the cinema, especially among the lower classes, was very strong and still developing. Some of the biggest names in the industry are associated with the DMK and many of the DMK's leaders have at times been active as writers and producers of films.

The economic factor, finally, also helps explain the DMK rise to power. Abandoning its separatist rhetoric in the 1960's, the DMK turned to bread and butter political issues. The years 1965 and 1966 were drought and food scarcity years, and prices at the time were in a continuously upward spiral. The 1967 DMK promise to provide, if elected, a cheap quality rice at a rupee a measure to all in need — a promise, incidentally, met only in Madras and Coimbatore and their satellite towns following the elections — attracted tremendous interest in the context of rising prices.

The images of Dravidian political movements are hardly as bright now as they were.[12] Few parties, if any, can achieve all that they promise before an election and the requirements of day-to-day administration have taken away some of the lustre the DMK party had when it came into power.

Yet, even since 1967, parties with "Dravidian" political orientations have continued to do well in Tamilnadu political life. Between 1967 and the end of 1971, the DMK fared well in most of the state's by-elections. It held its own in the 1970 *panchayati raj* elections. And it took 183 of the 234 Legislative Assembly seats and twenty-two of the state's thirty-two Lok Sabha seats in the March 1971 general elections.

Since the time of our field research in Chennanagar, towards the end of 1972, the DMK split into two factions, the splinter faction being headed by M.G. Ramachandran, popularly known as MGR, an aging but still very popular Tamil film star, an MLA, a well-known philanthropist and, before his break with the DMK regulars, the state treasurer of this party. The split has divided DMK forces (MGR's group is called the Annadurai DMK) but, for Tamilnadu, it does not yet seem to identify a decline in the popularity of Dravidian kinds of political interests.

In fact, by now the deceased Annadurai has been given the kind of acclaim many other heroes in India have attracted in the past.[13] His picture hangs in many homes and offices and is often garlanded and approached with special veneration. His memorial site along the Marina attracts thousands of visitors, and many of these approach the site with an attitude of religious pilgrimage. During his life-time, Annadurai came to stand for the hopes and aspirations of many of the common people. In his death he has assumed, for many, far more than life-size proportions.

The City

The city of Madras is also one of the fourteen districts in Tamilnadu. A district collector and his staff locally administer the state's interests and stand responsible for the collection of the state's share of revenue. Town planning, welfare and relief, rationing, and other state pro-grammes are coordinated through the collector's office.

At the same time, Madras has been (since 1688) and still is a corpo-ration. The city is divided into 120 electoral divisions (wards), each of which is represented to the municipal council by a councillor elected by adult franchise. The councillors elect a mayor. The corpo-ration has as executive head, a commissioner appointed by the state government. Councillors are elected for three-year terms and receive no salaries. They are provided only with small allowances for travel. Yet the position of councillor is eagerly sought for it puts successful competitors into positions of power and prestige.

In theory the corporation deals with all things that have to do with "...the health, safety, comfort and convenience of the citizens."[14] It deals with both obligatory functions — for example, the construc-tion and maintenance of roads, the vaccination of the population, and the supervision of public markets — and optional functions — for example, the reclamation of unhealthy lands, the development of public parks and gardens and the construction of poor houses.[15] The councillors are formally encouraged, in general, to call the atten-tion of proper authorities to any neglect in the execution of municipal activities and to suggest any improvements they consider desirable. But in practise the duties of the councillors boil down to the provision and maintenance of light, water, and sewage facilities in the areas for which they are responsible.

Like other Indian cities, Madras is beset by problems in develop-ment and administration. It faces a perenial shortage of funds.[16]

At the same time, the city's lower level office holders are almost completely entangled in the files and records of their offices. At higher levels, office holders are in a position to circumvent formal requirements and often expeditiously effect what they will. At lower levels, few officials are willing to take initiative on any matter. Mistakes can cost them their jobs, and jobs are scarce in Madras. Lines of authority and communication in government offices are well defined, but in practise it is difficult to follow them through.

The DMK was strong first in the cities of Tamilnadu, then in the state as a whole. Today the DMK controls the Madras Corporation as it does the state's Legislative Assembly.[17]

In addition to the elected and other officials in Madras, there are the organizations of the political parties. The larger parties — right now, the DMK and the Congress — have, as basic structural units, committees at the ward level. These tie in with committees at the circle (ten wards comprise a circle) and higher levels and, in turn, with party units at the state level. Other parties are similarly organized, where they have followers, to the extent possible. In all parties, funds are raised through membership fees and in charging admission to special events.

ELECTED LEADERS

The people of Chennanagar are involved in at least four general levels of elections. They are eligible to vote for candidates to the Indian parliament, the state Legislative Assembly, the municipal council, and local political associations (*manrams*).

The political horizons of most of the Chennanagar people, however, are very limited. Most are concerned so persistently with problems of food, shelter, and clothing that they have little direct interest in issues of state or national importance. Almost all the people know of such things as the Indo-Pakistani wars of the 1960's and the war involved in the emergence of Bangladesh, but few know their details. They know who is the Prime Minister of India but few can place precisely cities like Bombay and Delhi on a national map. The people pay attention to state politicians when they speak of slums, food prices, housing conditions, and corruption in office, for such problems directly concern them. They quickly lose interest when speakers turn to the more abstract interests of Tamilnadu as a state.[18]

Periods of elections in Chennanagar, insofar as they concern the people, cause a great deal of excitement. Public meetings at which influential leaders or celebrities describe the accomplishments and plans of the candidates generate much enthusiasm. Pamphlets are distributed. Posters giving the qualifications of the candidates, or party symbols and promises, are plastered on convenient surfaces. Processions to the accompaniment of drums, public address systems and slogan-shouting party faithfuls wind their way through the ward. If a film star like M.G. Ramachandran appears at a local meeting, thousands attend, and the candidate he supports gains a tremendous boost. To contain such an influence, an opposing party will call in an imposing figure to represent its side.

An excitement also develops around the electoral process because the spoils of election for both the victors and those who side with the candidates are important in and of themselves. Most of the people know that officials, especially those at the higher levels, have a great deal of power. They know officials are in a position to find jobs for others and help determine the distribution of big sums of money. Thus they seek — especially through their leaders — to find favour with the candidates for office and feel they have gained patrons to whom they can turn for special services should the persons they support gain election. For this reason, in part, elections for MP's and MLA's have so far caused much less direct enthusiasm in Chennanagar than have, for example, elections for municipal councillors. The constituencies involved in MP and MLA contests are large and the chances of the Chennanagar people and their leaders to gain effective personal relationships with the more powerful candidates are slight. The Chennanagar people only become involved in an indirect way. They get caught up in the excitement of the period but so far have had little to lose or gain here in the direct exercise of power. None of the contestants at this level have ever had close associations with the Chennanagar people.

Some of the many factors involved in the selection of candidates in the Chennanagar area can be identified in a brief review of the factors involved in the selection of a municipal council candidate. First, there is the matter of sex. No woman holds any elective position in Chennanagar and none ever has. The people know that India has a woman as Prime Minister but this does not alter their understandings of the place of women in local affairs. Women are locally considered to be politically inferior. They make less money, they are less likely to have an education, fewer of them read and write and no respectable woman ventures out by herself at night. Good women do as they are told. On election day, they go to the polling stations in groups and vote as their men tell them to vote.

A second factor involves income and occupation. According to estimates, the total sum of money municipal council candidates in Ward 21 (the ward to which Chennanagar belongs) today spend in their campaigns, ranges between Rs 3,000 and Rs 5,000. Expenses are involved in the hiring of taxis for special guests; the hiring of rickshaws, *bundies*, and lorries to haul supporters to the polls; the purchase of refreshments and gifts that candidates offer their helpers; the Rs 120 deposit required at the time of registration; and the money that must be spent in buying votes. In order to meet such expenses, a candidate must be well off himself or have access to people who are willing to help him. A person with a good income has a clear advantage.

Third, party affiliation is important. Chennanagar is a DMK slum. According to political leaders in Ward 21, the official candidate of a party can expect to receive about 90 per cent of the votes of those who belong to the party. In Chennanagar, where the few Congress supporters have not even been allowed to draw water locally, the percentage that votes DMK is at least this high.

Fourth, and most importantly, the successful candidate must demonstrate an ability to get things done. He may do this simply in relation to the contacts he has with important people. Or he may do this in the long run by performing the chores that put others in his debt. Many things are in scarce supply in Chennanagar and the people seek leaders who can bring them tangible results.

Among the other factors involved are caste and the payment for votes. Caste is still important but only in a general sense. A higher caste candidate who shows any public hesitancy in condemning claims of political superiority for higher caste groups would never be locally supported — the ideologies of the Dravidian movement have made at least this much of a local impact. At the same time, a Sudra or Untouchable candidate has an advantage in the area for these groups predominate and have learned to exercise the power the franchise gives them. More specific considerations of caste have little importance for the local electoral process. The buying of votes, meanwhile, can hardly push the electoral process too far out of regular channels, considering the factors already mentioned. "Tips" for votes can often sway the uncommitted into the ranks of those offering the money and an effective candidate knows how to pay. But many in Chennanagar would be embarrassed to receive payments for their votes. Among other things, an acceptance here puts them into a begging position in relation to which they can hardly expect to gain later in the more important advantages of a personal association. On the other hand, some are very poor and the Rs 2 to 4 generally offered for a promised vote is about equivalent to an average day's wages. Those who accept money, in any case, do so without embarrassment. They say: "Why shouldn't we? They get help when we vote for them. We should get something too."

The present councillor for Ward 21 embodies nicely many of the characteristics required of one who attains his position. He dresses well and lives in the ward. In the past, he has been a soldier, lorry driver, police constable, railway fireman, and cinder salesman, and in these positions has gained a breadth of practical experience and a good deal of financial independence. He began to take an active interest in politics at the time of national independence and claims that all along he has been interested in helping others. On his own, in 1963, he started a *manram* in Ambedkarnagar where he now lives. During the years he has served as president of this *manram* and has been able to nurture many associations with leaders in the area. He claims he has introduced a number of improvements in the ward and many support him in his claim. He has been resourceful and able to accomplish things for himself and for others. He is a Harijan by caste.

The only problem in understanding his election as councillor is that he is a member of the Congress in a ward that should have elected a DMK councillor in the 1968 elections. But this too falls into place for he was elected because of the split that occurred in the DMK pattern of voting when a strong DMK supporter challenged the party's official candidate. With about 60 per cent of the ward's 10,000 voters voting, the councillor received 2,500 votes while his two opponents, both DMK supporters, received 2,200 and 1,300 votes respectively.

Ward 21 has usually elected Congress representatives in the past, and the political influences of the Congress have left many traces. Most of the poor people know well the name Mahatma Gandhi and quickly associate it with the Congress and the interests of the socially disadvantaged. For them, the names of a number of neighbouring slums — for example, Bharatinagar, Nehrunagar, Indiranagar, and Gandhinagar — relate to Congress identities. Kamaraj Nadar, previously the chief minister of Madras and chairman of the all-India Congress Committee, has long been an attractive figure to many of the poor in Madras. Nevertheless, the Ward 21 area, like much of the rest of the city — and for the kinds of reasons earlier identified as underlying the DMK rise to power — has now become more and more inclined towards the DMK.

MANRAMS

When Chennanagar was first settled, local questions of order and control were in the hands of an informally defined *panchayat*.[19] This group consisted of some of the more influential early settlers and changed in composition from time to time, in relation to the issues under consideration. It dealt with problems such as the distribution of water, adultery, the reservation of space for a temple; and the settling of disputes between families. It also helped decide which people were permitted to move into Chennanagar. Unlike the *gram panchayats* and caste *panchayats* in villages, its areas of concern were never carefully understood.

Eventually, the informal *panchayat* was replaced by a *manram*. Today, three of these associations have been formed in Chennanagar for the purpose of securing basic amenities for their members. Supposedly, no *manram* has any direct political associations, but, in fact, each is identified with a particular party and almost all of their active members are active party members as well. Each of the *manrams* has a party flag in front of its headquarters, and pictures of party leaders and framed party manifestoes hang on the walls. No adult in Chennanagar has any difficulty in identifying the political affiliations of the different *manrams*.

The initial and largest *manram* in Chennanagar is the Chennanagar Kudisai Vazuvar Manram (The Chennanagar Hut Dwellers Association). This *manram* was founded shortly after most of the Chennanagar land was settled and grew out of the earlier *panchayat*. Its building stands at the first corner as one enters Chennanagar. A sturdy, mud-walled, thatch-roofed structure, one of its rooms is large enough to seat sixty to seventy people on the floor and is used for meetings. The other contains the bamboo poles and thatch matting used in constructing a platform for outdoor meetings, a caroms board for those who wish to play, and a steel cabinet containing the *manram's* records.

The Hut Dwellers Association provides water for its members and oversees the operation of the temple and the construction of the *nagar's* new latrines. It organizes the local commemoration of Annadurai's birthday and the Adi festival, and settles property disputes where possible. It raises money to rent public address systems, buy sweets for children, and pay for other items when public meetings are held. It is now saving money for a recreation-cum-marriage hall. It continues to work for the improvement of the local water supply, the transfer of formal land ownership to the people; and a local school, and it has been partially successful in the first two of these attempts. It has recently submitted a request to the mayor for more water and has been successful in getting the state government to send a surveyor to the *nagar* to define carefully the boundaries of each of the lots. The political relations of this association, historically and presently, side with the DMK. This party helped the people when they first settled the land, and this party has since helped them in many ways.

Officially, the Hut Dwellers Association has 376 members, one for each of the occupied houses in the *nagar*. Actually, only 320 households hold membership. *Manram* members pay membership fees of 60 n.p. a month. The proceeds go for the kinds of purposes already identified: Rs 40 per month to Arjuna Pillai, the priest; 25 n.p. per day towards the upkeep of the temple; oil for the *manram* lamps; Rs 1.50 per day as a tip to the driver of the lorry that brings the water; coffee and taxi fares for special guests, and so forth.

The leaders of the Hut Dwellers Association include a president, vice-president, secretary, treasurer, and sixteen councillors, two each for the eight streets in the *nagar*. The president is chosen by consensus and the attempt is made here to gain someone with as much influence as possible. K. Vezhavendam — Tamilnadu's Labour Minister during our period of research — was also this Association's president and the *manram's* members were very proud of this association. Vezhavendam had no specific responsibilities but was approached for special assistance when possible. The vice-president is responsible for the day-to-day activities of the *manram* and lives in the *nagar*.

Chennanagar's secretary and treasurer live outside Chennanagar but both have special local interests. The secretary, Subramaniam, was one of the initial settlers and owns a plot of land. His interests here are partially economic but, more importantly, also political. In serving Chennanagar as secretary and becoming known in nearby *nagars*, he can gain the attention of party leaders and build for himself a voting constituency, thus making it possible some day to stand for election. The treasurer, N. Raman, is responsible for keeping accounts and collecting membership fees. He and Subramaniam are both comparatively well-to-do and both have fairly wide reputations as reliable men in Korukupet.

The officers and street councillors of the Hut Dwellers Association, as of similar associations, are elected by the members. All members vote for vice-president, secretary, and treasurer; the street councillors are elected by the members who live on the respective streets. In the 1 March 1970 elections 216 of a possible 320 valid votes were cast. G. Narasimham obtained ninety-five votes to his two opponents' 106 votes (fifteen votes were declared invalid) to become vice-president; Subramaniam defeated his opponent by 116 to 100 votes; and Raman defeated his opponent by 136 to eighty votes. The elections at this level proceeded quite smoothly. The ideal pattern, however, seldom works in the election of councillors. Here, two men are usually co-opted from each street. In 1970, for example, no elections were held in seven of the streets. Only on the eighth street, where three men wanted to be representatives, was an election held.

The election of association officers caused some enthusiasm in Chennanagar. A good percentage (68 per cent in the 1970 elections) of the eligible voters vote and some of the contests are close. Much is at stake for those who want to become or remain politically active. On the other hand, the stakes are relatively small and often an election success is merely a formal stamp of approval given to an informal leader. As in higher level elections, the person given electoral backing here has a distinct advantage over those who contest on their own. What makes the situation different is that here new associations can easily be formed by leaders who are defeated in their bids for power or feel their groups are under-represented.[20] The two new Chennanagar *manrams* were formed out of the Hut Dwellers Association, under dissident leadership. Their formation took much of the contest out of the first *manram's* elections.

The second *manram*, the Chennanagar Makkal Natpani Manram (the Chennanagar People's Welfare Association), separated from the Hut Dwellers Association for a variety of reasons. According to the version of the parent association's leaders, M. Mariappan — an early settler of Chennanagar, one-time office holder in the Hut Dwellers Association and now secretary of the Welfare Association — arrogantly refused to abide by the parent association's rules and misappropriated the fees some of the members paid, reporting that they had not paid at all. Others say Mariappan disliked the parent association's sympathetic attitudes towards Harijans. According to Mariappan's version, leaders of the Hut Dwellers Association commonly used *manram* funds for personal purposes and often used the *manram* premises for drinking and gambling. Both versions are correct to some extent. However, the split occurred and two *manrams* with DMK leanings now do their best to attract support in Chennananagar. Mariappan formed his own *manram* when he was unable to make his way in the Hut Dwellers Association.

Like the first *manram*, the Welfare Association provides water for its members and is trying to help them in other ways. It runs a night school and claims that thirty children usually attend. Actually, the children meet very irregularly and seldom do more than five or six meet at one time. The organization of the Welfare Association is similar to that of the Hut Dwellers Association except that here there are twelve councillors elected at large from the membership of a 100. Though this *manram* has all the officers the first *manram* has, its local leadership rests largely in Mariappan's hands.

When the Welfare Association separated from the Hut Dwellers Association in 1968, many people opposed the split and the first attempt of the new association to set up headquarters met with disaster. The members of the first association pulled down the headquarters with the help of the police. Later, with the help of outside arbiters, the new *manram* gained the right of existence and, by now, animosities between the two associations have largely subsided. The relationship between them has reached a pass where the larger *manram* allows the smaller one freedom in performing its currently recognized duties. The Welfare Association collects its 50 n.p. dues from its members for the water they receive without opposition, and no one obstructs it in the services it provides. On the other hand, its attempts at expansion have been blocked. When it tried in June 1970 to set up a temporary structure on the land viewed by the first *manram* as a site for its planned meeting hall, with a view to building permanently later, the temporary structure was torn down by members of the first *manram*.

The third Chennanagar association, the Gandhi Sevak Sangh, also emerged out of the diversity of local political views, and despite the services the first two offered. As the name suggests, this *manram* has Congress affiliations. It was started on 22 March 1970, on the realization by Congress *nagar* residents that DMK supporters received more benefits than non-DMK supporters. Because of the split, the twelve households that now belong to this association have not been permitted to draw water nor to receive the other services provided in the *nagar*. Again, the reasons for this are numerous and the blame rests partly with the dissident households, for they consider it below their dignity to ask for assistance, and partly with the DMK *manrams* for they will not distribute anything to the Congress supporters without their humbly asking for it. However, Congress supporters are at a distinct disadvantage in Chennanagar.

The competition among the three Chennanagar *manrams* today revolves around their abilities to do things for their members. The Christian Council for Social Service, in constructing latrines in Annanagar, approached only the leaders of the main *manram*. The same Council distributes powdered milk and holds its public welfare meetings under the auspices of this *manram*. M. Mariappan of the Welfare Association, in response says the people feel the Hut Dwellers Association is really responsible for the services and that the people want to associate with this *manram* in order to benefit from the offered services. The members of the Hut Dwellers Association, meanwhile, encourage such notions and often refuse to give milk or allow attendance at public meetings to non-members. The identification here and in similar situations works to the benefit of the Hut Dwellers Association and to the disadvantage of the other *manrams*. *Manrams* serve as springboards into larger political arenas. To the extent a *manram* can accomplish things, it is successful in the eyes of the people and effective as a political base for its leaders.

GETTING THINGS DONE

The Chennanagar people are not yet sure they will be allowed to settle permanently on the land. Few of them have steady jobs and most are in debt to moneylenders. Their children have access to only the poor quality schools around and even essentials like water are in short supply. But despite such problems, almost none of the Chennanagar people exhibit the helplessness or hopelessness that many would ascribe to slum dwellers. There are many ways to do things here and in the past people have made use of established procedures while always devising new ways of accomplishing what they can.

On the one hand, they have done many things for themselves. They moved on to the land without legal right and claimed it, and, with their own collections of money, built a temple and employed a priest. They make use of their *manrams* and leaders. When they hear firms are hiring labourers, they go to them and apply for jobs. They go to hospitals in search of assistance when they need it. They know of some of the programmes the government has initiated for the development and clearance of slum areas and hope some of these improvements will affect them. Most adults have at times become intensely involved in the electoral process, recognizing that elected officials stand to profit by making good at least some of their campaign promises.

However, self-help is not always possible or even appealing as an alternative to many of the Chennanagar people. In their context, they not only lack material possessions but also power and influence. In modern Madras — where jobs, space, and goods are scarce — people often feel it is useless to wait in line for such things as advertised job openings. The competition for jobs, as for many other things, is almost always severe, and without some kind of help the Chennanagar people know that the chances are they will not be successful. At the same time, their experiences with officials in Madras have not been encouraging. Most of the lower level officials — the only levels with which the Chennanagar people can come into contact on their own — are impressively bogged down with paper work, and few of them have independent jurisdiction in any decision making area. They find it easy to confuse a Chennanagar person, sidetrack him, or bluntly refuse the requests he makes. It has become one of the principal functions of such officials to insulate higher level officials from the petitions people like those from Chennanagar bring. Decisions in the government and other bureaucracies of Madras are generally made only at the highest levels.

The feeling the Chennanagar people have that they can accomplish things does not come out of their feeling that they can demand things for themselves. It stems, rather, out of the understanding that any formal obstacle can be circumvented if one has the right patron or the right amount of money.

The important thing, then, is to find patronage. In this, the Hut Dwellers Association has been especially successful for at the time of

our research, it had as its president the Labour Minister of Tamilnadu. The Association could never directly demand the minister's
services for he had many other responsibilities, but he could be
approached for special services from time to time. For example,
when the Hut Dwellers Association sought to get more water for the
nagar, it first approached its president for a letter of recommendation.
Only then did it approach the city corporation for only then was it
guaranteed a respectful hearing.

For similar reasons, the other Chennanagar manrams have also
tried to gain the patronage of important figures. The current
president of the Welfare Association is an area lawyer who is prominent in DMK circles. The Gandhi Sevak Sangh does not yet have a
president but hopes to find suitable leadership soon. It has even
thought of developing some kind of direct association with Kamaraj
Nadar.

The workings of patronage are clear in many instances. When the
Welfare Association split off from the Hut Dwellers Association, it
was able to install and offer its membership a new supply of water
through the assistance of the councillor who, though a Congressman,
was one who saw in the split a chance to increase his local influence.
The councillor is routinely supposed to do such things as provide
water for the people, but no one in Chennanagar feels this was done
locally only in accord with duty. Thus the Welfare Association
claimed it had the support of the tahsildar before it tried to build a new
association building, and thus, only when the members of the Hut
Dwellers Association found the tahsildar was never even consulted,
did they tear down the structure.

Finally, because of the patronage they have, the people have persist-
ed in the illegal occupancy of the Chennanagar land and the hope of
being able to stay for a very long time. They seek patronage wherever
they can find it — through local leaders, outside contacts, elected
representatives, employers and so forth — and always feel confident
in an ambiguous situation if they have the support of a person with
influence.

Money, meanwhile, facilitates relationships where patronage is
weak or unavailable. The Chennanagar people commonly give a
little money on the side for such things as free vaccinations,
"permission" for their children to attend public schools, the guarantee
that their water will be delivered on time and in full, and the right to
be ushered by peons into public offices. Many of them explain that

the councillor will take bribes from them if they approach him for favours but are not members of his political organization or persons he is trying to get on his side. Many explain that they have to pay bribes for almost any kind of special service if they do not have contacts with people in a position to help them. The people have very little money, and they vocally condemn corruption. Nevertheless, almost none of them hesitates to use money when he feels it will be helpful to do so.

CONCLUSION

Harold A. Gould, recognizing the influences traditional features have on modern features in Indian political organization, has constructed what he calls a *jati*-model of Indian politics. He outlines it like this:

> The *jati*-model...is an operative feature of the mental life of most Indians. Its origin lies in the fact that most Indians are socialized in socio-religious *jatis* whose persistence depends upon the survival of the social structures and cultural values which support it. Its specific relevance is to group formation and participation. In many domains of modern Indian social life, including politics, where caste in its traditional forms is not a legitimized, sanctioned basis for role recruitment, patterning and inter-action, Indians tend to model the informal and *ex-officio* group structures which form and become the viable bases for determining power relations and reward distributions in these domains, on the principles of solidarity, reciprocity, exclusiveness and ethnicity which this *jati*-model codifies.[21]

Caste *per se* has little direct influence on the political processes of Chennanagar. Leadership is not correlated with caste and there is little evidence that political associations of any kind have emerged on the basis of caste. Yet a caste-like mentality and procedure governs political relationships. Those who seek to accomplish things do so primarily through patronage. They seek to establish personalistic ties.[22] Seldom, if ever, do they form associations in relation to ideological commitments. When they do things they do them for limited circles of friends and relatives and the patronage they seek is a limited patronage. In their relationships with patrons, the people can seldom make demands on the basis of right or precedent. Rather, involving only particular persons as such relationships do, particular questions are decided on the basis of their particular merits and hold good only for particular times. Their implications are not transferable.

In short, though political action in Chennanagar is by no means now a simple product of traditionally defined socio-religious groupings, the political interactions of the people can partially be understood with reference to some of the characteristic underpinnings of the Indian social order.

Simultaneously, newer forms of political organization also play a very vital role in Chennanagar. *Manrams*—in part formally constituted but also with distinctly developing, informally defined roles of their own — here have become platforms in relation to which the people make demands, determine their leadership, find their interests represented and relate themselves to "outside" political figures. Membership in these newer political forms is hardly voluntary, in one sense, given the fact that membership ties in so closely even with something as elementary as the need for potable water.

But membership in such associations also represents something very close to a very modern kind of political affiliation depending not at all on traditionally ascribed identifications. That is, a major system of organization here is via the political party and, in part, the local community is organized as a subgroup of a larger nationally or regionally defined, "voluntary" joined network, the political party. By virtue of this organization, some of the goods controlled by the state enter the local community for distribution. In return the party collects support (or votes).

To conclude, there is in Chennanagar a clearly developing political-ecological reciprocity. And this speaks well for the grass-roots authenticity of the modern Indian political process. The authenticity here, in fact, contrasts markedly with that occurring in other developing situations, for example, that occurring in the part of Latin America described by Lisa Peattie.[23]

REFERENCES

[1] For general analyses of the structure, problems, and character of government in India, see Richard L. Park, *India's Political System*, Prentice-Hall, Inc., Englewood Cliffs, New Jersey, 1967, and Norman D. Palmer, *The Indian Political System*, Houghton Mifflin Company, Boston, 1961.

[2] S.N. Eisenstadt, "Some Remarks on Patterns of Change in Traditional and Modern India," in K. Ishwaran (ed.), *Change and Continuity in India's Villages*, *op. cit.*, pp. 31-32.

[3] F.G. Bailey, *Politics and Social Change*, University of California Press, Berkeley, 1959.

[4] See Phillip Mason, "Unity and Diversity: An Introductory Review," *op. cit.*, pp. 1-29, and Hugh Tinker, "Is There an Indian Nation," in Phillip Mason (ed.), *India and Ceylon: Unity and Diversity*, *op. cit.* pp. 279-296.

[5] The best general summary of the Dravidian Movement's emergence and character is Robert L. Hardgrave, Jr., *The Dravidian Movement*, *op. cit.* See also P.D. Devanandan, *The Dravida Kazagham: A Revolt Against Brahminism*, Christian Institute for the Study of Religion and Society, 1960.

[6] See S.N. Balasundaram, "The Dravidian (Non-Brahmin) Movement in Madras," in Iqbal Narain (ed.), *State Politics in India*, Meenakshi Prakashan, Meerut, 1967, p. 171.

[7] See Robert L. Hardgrave, "Religion, Politics and the DMK," *op. cit.*, p. 230.

[8] On the change here see C.N. Annadurai, "DMK as I see It," in Iqbal Narain (ed.), *State Politics in India*, *op. cit.* For a balancing view see also S.N. Balasundaram, "The Dravidian (Non-Brahmin) Movement in Madras," *op. cit.*

[9] See Richard L. Park, *India's Political System*, *op. cit.*, p. 65.

[10] See Robert L. Hardgrave, *The Dravidian Movement*, *op. cit.*, p. 8.

[11] On the general characteristics of elites in India and the gap between the elites and the common people, see T.B. Bottomore, "Modern Elites in India," in T.K.N. Unnithan, Indra Dev, and Yogendra Singh (eds.), *Towards A Sociology of Culture in India*, Prentice-Hall of India, Ltd., New Delhi, 1965, chapter 9, and S.N. Eisenstadt, "Some Remarks on Patterns of Change in Traditional and Modern India," *op. cit.*

[12] In fact, P. Spratt (*DMK in Power*, Nachiketa, Bombay, 1970) claims the DMK's performance in office is hardly distinguishable from that of the predecessor Congress government. On this, see also Mythily Shivaraman, "The Dravida, Munnetra Kazagham: The Content of its Ideology," *The Radical Review*, I Madras, 1970.

[13] For a blunt overstatement on this see Agehananda Bharati, "Hinduism and Modernization," in Robert Spencer (ed.), *Religion and Change in Contemporary Asia*, University of Minnesota Press, Minneapolis, 1971.

[14] J.C. Molony, *A Book of South India*, Methuen and Co. Ltd., London, 1926, p. 141.

[15] See Chetkar Jha, *India's Self Government*, Patna, 1953, pp. 40-42.

[16] In terms of economic development, India is in a transition from a backward economy into a self-sustaining economy. Economic growth has so far been below

expectations, but the elements of the infrastructure of economic development are constantly being strengthened. Yet such sources as the Tamilnadu Directorate of Town Planning (1970-71) and V.M. Dandekar and N. Rath'("Poverty in India") *op. cit.* make it clear there are plenty of economic problems remaining in Madras and other Indian urban centres.

[17] Of 120 councillors in Madras in June 1970, fifty-four belonged to the DMK, forty-seven to the "Old" Congress, seven to the Muslim League, five to the "New" Congress three to the Swatantra, and one each to the Right Communists, Left Communists, TAK, and Toilers Party. The six co-opted councillors then serving on the council (if a circle does not have at least one council or of Scheduled Caste background, one is co-opted from such circles to the council, through election by the councillors) were all of the DMK, bringing the total number of DMK councillors to sixty.

[18] F. Bailey (*Politics and Social Change, op. cit.,* pp. 88) says: "Of their own accord very poor people take part in politics, nor is it easy to organize them for political action. They remain interested in the welfare of themselves and their families and will not spare time or energy to work for the collectivity."

[19] For a brief statement on the place of the *panchayat* in village social organization, see John Adams and Uwe J. Woltemade, "Village Economy in Traditional India: A Simplified Model," *Human Organization,* 29 (Spring), 1970.

[20] Only seven members are required for a society to be registered according to the Registration of Societies Act, Tamilnadu.

[21] Harold A. Gould, "Toward a Jati-Model for Indian Political Relations," in *Economic and Political Weekly,* IV, 1 February 1969.

[22] See F.G. Bailey, *Politics and Social Change, op. cit.,* pp. 141-157.

[23] Lisa R. Peattie, *The View from the Barrio,* University of Michigan Press, Ann Arbor, 1968.

Seven

Religion

The distribution of the 376 Chennanagar heads of households by general religious identification is as follows: Hindu, 363; Christian, nine; Muslim, four. Thus most of the material that follows will have to do with Hinduism as it is locally organized. After a general description of the religious context, this chapter will analytically describe aspects of practical Hinduism in Chennanagar and certain perspectives of local Hinduism.

THE CONTEXT

Hinduism, of course, is the dominant religious system in India and Tamilnadu and, by far, it is the dominant religious system in Madras. Census figures for 1961 give the distributions, by religious identification, of the populations in India, Tamilnadu, and Madras, as follows (Table 7.1).

Table 7.1

DISTRIBUTION BY RELIGION OF THE INDIA, TAMILNADU, AND MADRAS POPULATIONS (BY PER CENT)

Religion	India	Tamilnadu	Madras
Hinduism	83.5	89.5	85.0
Islam	10.7	4.1	7.5
Christianity	2.4	5.2	6.9
Other	3.4	0.2	0.6

Source : Census of India, 1961.

As in most other parts of India, Hinduism manifests itself in Madras in rich diversity. Many missions, associations, and colleges here teach the great cultural traditions of Hinduism. Holy men and pilgrims pass labourers, beggers, and businessmen along the streets and are as integral a part of the city as are any of the latter. Fortune tellers and magicians of a sometimes confusing variety but, in most cases, in some ways concerned with certain Hindu teachings and mythologies, serve those who seek their insights. *Disti bomas* (human images that ward off an "evil eye") are hung on both private and public buildings under construction. Though some people now hang these dolls for tradition's sake alone, many continue to hang them with a view to warding off the covetous glances of those with evil intentions. Many taxi and bus drivers, for their talismanic effect put pictures and icons of their favoured deities on the dashboards and sun-visors of their vehicles. New vehicles are often dedicated in the name of a particular deity. To honour the deities of the temples they pass, some passers-by appropriately touch themselves or do *namaste*. The names of firms, as the names of people, often identify them with particular religious figures, and you can find such commodities as Ganesh *beedis* for sale and such service companies as the Venkateshwarluswami bus lines in the city.

Madras has never been a major temple or pilgrimage centre. Nevertheless, its position within the sacred geography of Hinduism is important.[1] The historic Siva and Vishnu temples of Mylapore and Triplicane, respectively, have long been patronized by great numbers of people and they are very actively patronized today. Madrasis also visit the various other major and minor temples of the city. Approximately 300 of these are served by boards of trustees. In addition, there are innumerable kinds of sidewalk, slum, and neighbourhood temples.[2]

The Madrasis also visit temples in other parts of the state and many go on pilgrimages to religious and cultural centres in different parts of India.[3] The pilgrimage centres of Tirupati, Kanchipuram, Rameshwaram, Tirutani, Madurai, and Kanyakumari are all easily accessible from Madras.

Religion and Society in India

It has been found impossible to distinguish clearly between the "religious" and "secular" spheres of life in most rural Indian contexts.[4] In the ideal-typical village, indeed, religion pervades all aspects of life and it matters here how and where one builds his house, how one addresses his superiors, clothes himself, marries, eats, and works. It also matters here how one conducts himself in every aspect of life, for much of what is specifically "right" and "wrong" for an individual can be related to the moral code applicable for his caste. The standards of the individual's performance with respect to the requirements of his position determine his acceptability in this life and his standing in future lives.[5]

No village in India knows the complete integration of the religious and the secular that the above description implies. In all villages, some people are known to be more religious than others, identified as such in their special abilities, special care for temples, extra devotion to particular deities, and upright moral behaviour.

Then too, the above description — a description from a social organizational perspective — is only one perspective of Hinduism and, though important, it disallows a look at the cultural traditions of Hinduism as independent from the system of social organization. In fact, the great and little traditions of Hinduism have been found to have an understandable reality apart from the organization of caste in the rural Indian context. Relatedly, most scholars would agree with M. Marriott that the religious traditions of the village may be conceived

...as resulting from continuous processes of communication between a little, local tradition and greater traditions which have their places partly inside and partly outside the village. Only residual fragments of the religion of such a little community can be conceived as distinctive or separable.[6]

But whatever the separability of the traditions of Hinduism from the Indian system of social organization, it is also true that these traditions reinforce the system of caste, and vice versa. Processes such as those involved in Sanskritization — where a caste's hierarchical position in relation to local and regional caste contexts depends at least to some extend on the quality of its attributes, as these may be evaluated in the light of great traditional understandings — link the caste system to Hinduism's cultural traditions.[7] Contrariwise, at least certain of the religious beliefs and practices in a village context can be roughly correlated with caste groupings at different levels and it is generally true that the highest castes are more attuned than the lower with the great traditions of Hinduism, and the lower than the higher with the little traditions of Hinduism. To put things differently, in ways the caste system can be considered the "church of Hinduism."[8]

Caste considerations are much less important in Madras than they are in the villages of the area. As we have noted earlier, such considerations have been (i) structurally undermined, as modern means of transportation and communication and new housing and industrial programmes have been introduced, and (ii) ideologically undermined, in relation to such influences as the anti-Brahmin teachings of the DMK, an increasing secularism, and the increasingly technological and urban orientations of many of the people.

Such influences have also affected the local understandings of Hindu traditions. The DMK's negative evaluations of Hinduism, for example, have led to a popular atheism among some of the movement's leaders and to such striking manifestations of anti-Hinduism as the perversion of certain Sanskrit epics. To illustrate, E.V. Ramaswamy Naicker wrote and published in 1959 a distortion of the *Ramayana* in which Ravana, the villian by common interpretation, becomes a Dravidian hero. The general claim by DMK leaders has been that Hinduism in the South is an import from the North that dulls the senses of the masses in its ideologies, while at the same time limiting their aspirations through its correlated system of stratification.[9]

However, as we have seen, caste considerations remain basically important in Madras, and the ideological renaissance of Hinduism, a renaissance generally noticed in recent decades,[10] is coupled in Madras with a practical resurgence in Hindu beliefs and practices. Regarding the latter of these points, first, the proliferation of temples in Madras is continuous and more people now visit more of these than ever before, in the process giving more than ever before.[11] Second, there has been in Madras a continuous development of religious groupings and associations that are little, if at all, correlated with caste considerations. Such associations can be found in rural areas, of course, and they have always been possible within the generous ideological limits of Hinduism.[12] But in Madras, as in other urban centres, the proliferation of such associations is increasingly apparent.[13] Third, the notion that an "outside" religious system might someday replace Hindu ideologies is now in ruins.[14]

Islam and Christianity

Islam and Christianity constitute proportionately small percentages of the Madras population but both have many adherents and both have a long history in South India. Muslims started to come to the South in large numbers, in the thirteenth through fourteenth centuries. Today many of them are concentrated in the Thousand Lights and Royapettah areas of Madras though they are also scattered throughout the city. Most of the Muslim heads of households in Madras are employed as petty shopkeepers, tailors, hide merchants, and labourers.

According to tradition, St. Thomas founded the Christian Church in South India in the first century of our era.[15] Today, however, there are more than 300 churches in Madras. These range, in size from the little thatch churches in the slums to the architecturally impressive St. Andrew's Cathedral in Vepery; in procedures, from the highly emotional services of little Pentecostal groupings to the formal services, conducted entirely in English, held in some of the larger churches. As in the rest of India, by far the majority of the converts to Christianity in Madras have come originally from the lowest castes only and the Church here is not an evangelical body now. Its activities, furthermore, are limited in various ways by caste, linguistic, regional, and background considerations.[16]

The Madras communities of Hindus and Muslims are relatively distinct. Localized flare-ups concerning such things as the location of mosques sometimes occur. But in general, though many of the interests of these two communities overlap, in most intimate social ways the two remain quite independent of each other.

The Christian community, meanwhile, to a large extent has been structurally absorbed within the framework of Hindu social organization. In the process, it has become relatively impotent practically, while still retaining meaningful influences ideologically. The latter is especially the case if considered in relation to the meetings and dialogues rather than the hostilities between the East and the West.[17]

The influences of Jainism, Buddhism, secularism, nationalism and so on contribute to the ideological and organizational complexities of the Madras religious context.

ASPECTS OF PRACTICAL HINDUISM IN CHENNANAGAR

Temple Worship

The Chennanagar temple is not in very good condition. The twelve by twelve foot structure, first erected in 1966 when the *nagar* was settled, is beginning to lean precariously. But then the Chennanagar temple does not play too important a part in the local round of activities.

Situated on the left side of the road into Chennanagar, the temple building was constructed at a cost of Rs 600. Its principal deity, Mariatha, the goddess of smallpox and other diseases similar in effect,[18] is represented on a platform in the centre of the temple by a two-foot idol. It is coloured with turmeric and vermillion and decorated with *neem* tree leaves. A brass lamp stand, a bell, and a conch shell are located near the idol. To the left as one enters the temple stands a six-inch image of Lord Ganesh. Representing prudence and sagacity, this deity is regularly invoked by worshippers before they approach Mariatha. He is also honoured at the beginning of many other undertakings. To the right stand two bricks coloured again with turmeric and vermillion and representing Lord Muneswaran, one of the forms of Lord Siva. The back wall of the temple is largely covered with framed pictures of the deities Lakshmi, Saraswati, Vishnu, Siva and Parvati, Ganesh, Venkateshwarlu, and Murugan. Hanging from the ceiling are three or four miniature cradles tied by women who have wished for but have not yet borne children.

The priest of the Chennanagar temple is Arjuna Pillai. Born in Kerala, he moved to Madras eighteen years ago. He married in Madras but his wife is now dead. Of his four children, he knows the whereabouts of only the young son with whom he now lives and the married daughter who also lives in Chennanagar.

Before becoming a priest, Arjuna Pillai rolled *beedis* and had little formal interest in Hinduism. When his wife died, he decided to lead a saintly life and devoted himself to the teaching of religion. He dresses today in simple white clothing, wears his hair shoulder length, and is called "*swami*" (the popular appellation for a holy man) by the people. Though he is not of a priestly caste — he is a Kanakka Pillai — Arjuna Pillai was called by the first *panchayat* of Chennanagar to serve as the *nagar's* priest. The *panchayat* members had heard of his exemplary life in Washermenpet, his former home.

Arjuna Pillai offers both morning and evening prayers at the temple, keeps the temple clean, and is responsible for assisting in the worship conducted there. He also assists in the performance of certain of the rituals associated with local ceremonies and sells medicines and charms to ward off devils, restore health, encourage success and so forth. He

lives off the Rs 40 he gets monthly from the principal Chennanagar *manram* — payment for his services as priest as well as for his
help in keeping track of this *manram's* distribution of water — plus
the payments in cash and kind he receives for any special services he
offers the people. He gets 25 n.p. a day from the *nagar's* main *manram*
with which to buy flowers and the other things he needs for the temple.

About twenty people visit the Chennanagar temple on an average
Friday, the day auspicious for Mariatha. On other days, except
during festivals or special family observances, the number of visitors
seldom exceeds five or six.

The two special celebrations observed at the Chennanagar temple
occur during the month of Adi, the month most significant in the
worship of Mariatha, and during Pongol. Prior to 1969, blood
sacrifices were offered during Adi. These, however, have now been
discontinued. In the words of Arjuna Pillai: "They were too grue-
some anyway and by now we know that such sacrifices are not
necessary."

The Chennanagar temple is in poor repair and proportionately
very few of the *nagar's* people visit it regularly. But temple
worship, in general, is important for almost all. First, all of them
know of the major pilgrimage centres in the area and have already
made a visit to one or would if they could, or if they had an
important enough reason to go. They go for reasons such as the
desire to bear children, pass examinations, regain health, and retain
health. They also go to worship and bring honour to the deities.

Few people expect all the requests they make will be granted. Yet
almost all go with the knowledge, borne by legend after legend, that
the powers of the deities associated with particular temples are
immense. They also go in the knowledge that the visit itself is a
meaningful event in the religious life of a person. Finally, of course,
they go for the trip itself, now made more and more convenient in
relation to improved facilities for transportation and accommodation. Such journeys are often pleasureable and the activities at the
pilgrimage centres are usually as meaningful in the festive as in the
religious senses.[19]

Second, temple worship is important for the majority of the people
in that most of them visit at least certain temples from time to time.
Each of the slums around Chennanagar has a little temple of its own.
Two miles down the Erukancheri Road is the Shri Srinivasa Perumal
temple of Lord Vishnu.[20] The people pass the many temples of the

city as they move about and all of them know about the city's major
temples. Proportionately few — in the estimates of some of the local
leaders, perhaps 10 to 15 per cent — of the Chennanagar people are
regular in their visits to temples. Yet, in that temples are accessible
to the people in all parts of the city and in that the people do visit
them when they want to or feel that they should, without embarrassment, temple usage is an integral part of their religious life.

Third, the people want to have a temple in Chennanagar. They
already are collecting money for a new, more elaborate structure,
and they proudly plan for its erection.

Household Worship

All but twenty-three of the Chennanagar homes have a small
place for household worship. Here, commonly, there are several
pictures of favoured deities, a little niche with an oil burning lamp
and perhaps a little brass icon or two. During festival times,
especially, the floor in this part of the house is carefully smeared
with a cow-dung mixture and on this surface a design is drawn with
lime powder. Many families daily light an oil lamp in their worship
corner. Many regularly make small offerings to their deities and some
burn incense before and garland with flowers the representations of
their deities. A few of the people faithfully recite Sanskritic and
other chants in their homes. Most of the people, on the other hand,
only approach their deities on special occasions or in relation to
special wants and needs.

A few families daily put aside a little money as an offering to their
deities, depositing this in the temple of their choice from time to time.
During Adi, almost every Chennanagar family prepares a little
porridge as an offering to Mariatha, either in thanks for preventing
the illnesses for which she is responsible or in supplication for help.
The porridge is poured into a common vessel before the deity, then
distributed among the children. Some families save money, then
have *archanas* (ritual chants) performed for them. For example, they
might go to a particular temple to have the wedding of a deity
performed or the different names of a favoured deity chanted in
return for their money. In such ways they can accumulate the merit
that accrues to them through this kind of performance.

Life-Cycle Ceremonies

Principal life-cycle ceremonies[21] — for example, those related to birth, naming, puberty, marriage, the birth of a first child, and death — are generally more carefully observed in relatively un-changing societies than in societies more subject to change. Rites of passage mark periods of transition, and the more unchanging the society, the more ascribed rather than achieved are the rights and responsibilities of member individuals at particular stages of life.

Chennanagar's patterns of community life are still relatively un-clear and will never become as carefully defined as they are in the rural Indian setting. However, all of the special occasions in the human life-cycle are observed here by at least some of the people. The obser-vances vary greatly in cost (as described in Chapter Five), number of persons involved, and ritual detail, but in general they continue to be important. All of them are in part reinforced by religious considerations and together they make up an important part in the local practice of Hinduism. Some notes on naming, ear-boring, puberty, marriage, and death ceremonies are given below.

Where possible, the naming ceremony commonly takes place in the home of the child's maternal grandmother, especially in the case of the birth of a first child. Otherwise, it takes place at the parents' home or at a temple. Usually, it occurs on the seventh, fourteenth, or twenty-eighth day after birth and doubles as a purification ceremony for the child and its mother. Generally, the name given the child is selected with the assistance of a priest familiar with the child's horo-scope, and a priest is usually invited to the home in order to purify it with sacred water before the occasion. The ceremony involves only intimate relatives and friends and some sharing of food. The uncles and maternal grandparents of the child usually give it presents at the ceremony, perhaps a pair of anklets or bangles.

The ear-boring ceremony has lost its religious meanings for almost all the Chennanagar people. Yet, sometime during childhood the ears of most children are pierced. Uusually, the hair of the children involved is offered as a sacrifice to the deity of the household at the time of the ceremony.

Puberty ceremonies have lost much of their significance among many of the higher caste and class groups in the Madras population.[22] But in Chennanagar, as in many other lower class Madras settings, a puberty ceremony for females is still often observed. It announces a girl's "coming of age" — her marriageability — and is usually observed on the fifth day after menstruation begins. Female relations are invited to join the celebrations and they do so, heartily. Special dishes are prepared and the girl is given new clothes and jewelry.

Traditionally conducted marriages — and almost all Chenna-nagar are of this type — involve religious considerations at every stage of planning and participation. Usually, the parents of a boy of marriageable age, either by themselves or with the help of a third party, seek out a suitable bride. When such a girl is found, the horoscopes of the couple are examined by a priest to determine the suitability of the match. If the match is suitable in such terms (and in terms of all the other social, economic, and personal considerations involved), the engagement is formalized, the days and times of the nuptial events being determined in relation to the special "good" and "bad" times of the day, the "good" and "bad" times of the month, the positions of the prospective partners in their respective families and so forth. At all times, auspicious signs are happily recognized while inauspicious signs and happenings are avoided or counter-balanced where possible.

The kinds of gifts offered the marriage couple, the order in which they are offered, the kinds of leaves and the colors used to decorate betrothal and marriage day *pandals*, the order in which various members of the bride's and bridegroom's parties visit the temple before the final ceremony, the order of the ceremony itself: all these, to some extent, are determined by tradition alone. Yet, for most of the same, there is also an associated meaning that can be given in religious terms. The marriage ceremony takes place at a temple and the rituals associated with the ceremony are performed by priests.

The Chennanagar Christians and Muslims commonly bury their dead, while the others cremate them. The *padai* (platform) on which the corpse is transported to the cremation grounds is decorated with flowers. Musicians, or at least someone blowing on a conch shell, walk in front of the procession; the *padai* is usually carried by male relatives of the deceased; the mourners walk behind. Some-times, betel-nut leaves, *pori*, and flowers are scattered as the procession moves along.

On the day after death (or two or three days after), it is common for relatives and friends to go to the cremation or burial grounds with coconuts, water, and fruits and to offer these on behalf of the deceased. *Pujas* are also performed at this time. Commonly, on the fifteenth day following death, those directly involved in the funeral observances take purificatory baths and participate in a brief memorial service under the auspices of a priest. On the sixteenth day, relatives are invited for a feast.

PERSPECTIVES

Divergent Influences

Divergent influences constantly impinge on Chennanagar. The anti-Hindu, anti-Brahmin, and anti-religious teachings of the DMK have left an impact, and whatever the levels of understanding of these by the people — and however much these teachings have changed over time — many people are aware of the secular emphases of the movement.

Priests from other than the Brahmin caste have always been used by various groups in India, especially by those more cut off from the higher levels of the social and religious orders. But in Chennanagar, for example, though many people continue to use the services of Brahmin priests, even people from those groups commonly served almost exclusively by Brahmins in more traditionally organized areas now turn readily to non-Brahmins for assistance. They often use DMK kinds of arguments in justification of their changing preferences. The Chennanagar priest is a non-Brahmin; so are most of the other priests in this general area of Madras. At a particular village ceremony still carried out in some parts of Andhra Pradesh, Brahmin priests go from door to door, accepting gifts and homage in the names of the deities they represent, in return channelling blessings to the households. Recollecting this, one Telugu informant remarked simply: "That could never happen here."

Along similar lines, no matter how persistent the strengths of caste and the appreciation of the people for it, many now speak strongly against caste, often backing up their statements with references to DMK teachings.

Another of the impinging influences is that concomitant with technological, scientific, and related kinds of developments. And the effect here is sometimes dramatic. To illustrate, one young man, when asked if he had any faith in religious beings or superstitious practices, said: "When two Americans walked on the moon, I lost my belief in God. Before this, I did worship from time to time. But now? Do you expect me to do the same?"

Sarcastically, but with interspersed uproarious laughter, another informant, not educated formally but very insightful, said: "A childless wife will go to pray to a *neem* tree in order to conceive. She believes her prayers will be answered. But decide for yourself. Is the *neem* tree responsible? Is God responsible? Or is the husband responsible?"

Another influence, and one which counterbalances in ways the deleterious effects on local Hinduism of various modern developments, is that of the "resurgent" Hinduism commented upon earlier in this Chapter.

Writing of changes in village religious beliefs and practices in India, I have noted that lower caste persons are usually more convinced than their upper caste fellows that their religious orientations are in a state of decay. I explained the situation as follows.[23] Lower caste people are economically, politically, socially, and religiously more limited to the local village context than their upper caste fellows and are thus more out of contact with certain recent trends — for example, the increasing popularity of visits to pilgrimage centres; the increasing popularization of particular, more widely-known deities (for example, Vishnu, Ganesh, Lakshmi, and Saraswati) in relation to modern forms of communication, the cinema and so forth; and the increasingly standardized conceptualizations of moral behaviour over wide areas. They tend to see such things as an increasing skepticism concerning goddesses, spirits, and super-stitions, and a decrease in some of the definitive characteristics of local religious beliefs and practices, as indicative of a decline in the significance of religion in local affairs. On the contrary, higher caste people, more familiar as they are with the regional context, tend to view things differently.

A good number of the Chennanagar people do feel religion is less important now than it once was. Yet the Madras context is such that almost none of them can remain unaware of the ways in which Hinduism has been popularized, in the regional sense, in recent years. And certainly, such understandings influence the perspectives they have of their situation.

Understandings

Many traces of the great cultural traditions of Hinduism and their influences can be found in Chennanagar. In the mornings, three or four heads of households chant certain Sanskrit *mantras* and under-stand their meanings. Arjuna Pillai explains that when he sees "...a leper, a blind man, or a cripple," he thinks of "...*karma*, of what a person might have done in a previous life to deserve his present misfortunes." The deities pictured in the Chennanagar temple and in homes can all be related to stories in the sacred texts of Hinduism.

One of our Chennanagar friends told us: "Most of the people here do not understand how the worship of gods and spirits is related to an understanding of ultimate things, but maybe their understandings are good enough for them now. And maybe their understandings will develop."

However, and despite the fact most of them might not be able to relate their ideas to principles such as those that characterize the higher levels of Hinduism, most know their beliefs and practices can be meaningfully interpreted by others they consider more informed in matters of religion. Few of them categorically denounce any aspect of their general religious context.

In relation to this kind of relativism, few of the people are hesitant to speak of their religious understandings. At the same time, this relativism results in considerable variation in their explanations of things like the purposes of deities, man's relationship to his environment and the meanings of life. For example, concerning the possibility of life after death, some of our respondents commented:

After a person dies, if he has done wrong, he is punished. If not, I don't know what happens.

My *jeevurdu* will then be in the air, or in the mountains, or in the valleys. Or [pausing], why don't you tell me where it will be?

I don't know what happens after death and I don't care.

Those who live good lives are rewarded and those who live bad lives are tied up in chains, cut with saws, and burned with oil.

Is there a reward for being good? I don't know and I'm not interested in such things. I do not perform *pujas* regularly and I do not visit temples. There must be a God who created things but I won't spend money on Him and waste time doing *pujas*. I will try to do good things and avoid doing bad things. I will try not to cause pain to anyone. Anyway, man is visible and God isn't. Why shouldn't I believe more in someone like Gandhi than something like God?

After death, a person will be reborn in one form or another depending on what kind of life he lives now.

Most of the people know that justice, truthfulness, patience, reason, and the pursuit of wisdom are encouraged in their cultural traditions. And most of them consider themselves to be religious whatever their arguments against religion. The man above quoted as saying he lost his belief in God after the first Apollo landing on the moon, for example, also said that visits to pilgrimage centres are useful in obtaining the help of God. He said:

> I never visited Tirupati until the age of eighteen, though my parents went several times during my youth. When I finished eighth class, I went in search of a job but could find nothing. Then my parents told me: 'Go to Tirupati and within twelve days you will find a job.' I didn't want to go, but I did, thinking at least I should try what they suggested. Then, after twelve days, I got a job. I would now go to Tirupati anytime if I had a very special reason.

Hinduism allows for a wide variety in ideological terms, as can be observed in Chennanagar. Secular and other influences have penetrated here. But none of these have radically displaced local religious interpretations. Rather, little concerned with logical inconsistencies in the ways in which they understand their religious worlds, most of the people have simply accepted new interpretations in various areas of experience, at the same time continuing to accept the possibility, and reality, of other interpretations. In short, the people here (except, of course, for the few local Christians and Muslims) readily identify themselves as Hindus whatever their ideological diversities.

The concerns of most of the people, however, are much less directed towards the achievement of comprehensive levels of understanding than with the attempt to provide for themselves here and now. Thus, the reasons they give for such things as visits to pilgrimage centres or temples are commonly given in terms of the need to accomplish specific things, to satisfy particular desires, or to placate particular deities; seldom are they given more abstractly. Thus, when asked why people visit the temple in Chennanagar, the priest somewhat facetiously explained: "They come to pray for good marriages. They come to ask for better health and for the health of relatives who are sick. And they come with their lottery tickets, praying for a lucky draw and vowing they will build a new temple with some of the money, if they win."

In turn, the understandings of the people also relate to understandings of spirit worlds and magical practices. Many charms are used for assistance and to ward off possible dangers. Children, for protection or luck, often wear a black string brought from a pilgrimage centre or temple, perhaps with a small picture of a deity attached. Others do so too. In many bazaars it is possible to buy *taittulu* (little pieces of tin rolled up and containing something from a pilgrimage centre) which, if worn around the wrist, upper arm, or neck, can restore strength, give health, guarantee safety, or even assist one's intellectual powers. Those with animals sometimes mark them specially for their protection. All of the people know that "good" and "bad" signs can be identified, that certain plants grown near to homes are often grown with the intent of warding off possible dangers, that the characteristics of one's life can be interpreted in relation to happenings in the heavens and so forth. And, though not all of them believe these things for themselves, all of them know many who do.

A family with a kidnapped son — or one who had run away from home — was told by a gypsy fortune-teller that the son would return if the family faithfully tied, once a day for a month, little pieces of paper with religious sayings written on them, to the branches of the *neem* tree near their house. The family did this, knowing it was doing something that could bring the son back.

Meanwhile, many other such things are done and while some people are sarcastic in reference to their efficacy, most at least see no harm in doing them and quite commonly agree that desired results can sometimes thus be effected.

With reference to spirit beliefs, one of our most trusted informants estimated that about 90 per cent of the people believe in ghosts and spirits, in one way or another. Supposedly, the spirit of a young man who hanged himself near the outskirts of the *nagar* still appears from time to time. Some contend the *nagar* is haunted by numerous spirits, claiming that before it was settled, many murders were committed in this outlying part of town and that the spirits of the murdered still move in the area. Many believe sudden illnesses, sudden deaths, barrenness, and so on can be caused by the activities of spirits.

CONCLUSION

To sum up: (*i*) the religious context in which the people are involved is multi-faceted, and divergent influences constantly impinge on Chennanagar; (*ii*) though many of the more abstract-level teachings of Hinduism do penetrate Chennanagar, most people generally have much more mundane concerns; (*iii*) the religious worlds perceived by the people are inhabited by beings that can be conceived at a number of different levels and include conceptualizations of deities and higher level gods and goddesses as well as spirits, people with "evil eyes" and so forth; (*iv*) the people use "magical" as well as "religious" approaches in their coming to terms with the contexts in which they are involved; and (*v*) the ceremonies in which the people participate they often explain in relation to religious considerations.

On the one hand, then, little as well as great traditional religious influences — both "high" and "low" religious forms — characterize the Chennanagar ideological setting. And all of these currently tend to persist alongside each other, none really persisting at the expense of the others.

On the other hand, what of the relations between caste and its religious underpinnings? The answer to this question cannot be precise for organizational forms are still emerging in Chennanagar. Clearly, the local organization of beliefs and practices cannot be closely correlated with caste affiliations. But at the same time, the identifications of the people with caste remain important, for along with caste considerations go considerations of what is "right" and "wrong" for both the individual and his children. To illustrate (and here again is the kind of example earlier used in the discussion of caste in Chennanagar), a local astrologer, whose wife died about ten years ago and who now lives with a lower caste mistress, explained his situation like this:

> Yes, caste is important. I wanted to marry again after my first wife died, but according to my horoscope, I would never again have had a successful marriage. And so I did not remarry. Instead, I decided to live with this woman [referring to his mistress]. She does not belong to my caste. But with her I now have five boy children. When these boys are ready for marriage, they will not be able to find brides in my caste. We will have to look for brides for them in mixed caste families or in families where the parents are not married.

The rules of family life in Chennanagar still correlate in ways with caste considerations. So do ideas of what should be done. The religious life of Chennanagar blends into that of its surroundings. It lends an explanatory depth to local life; at the same time, its relations to social organization persist.

REFERENCES

[1] See Milton Singer, "The Great Tradition in a Metropolitan Centre," in *Journal of American Folklore*, 71 (July-September 1958).

[2] Our figures for the number of temples served by trustees, and the generalizations given here, were obtained in an interview with the Deputy Director of the Hindu Religious Endowment Board, Madras, on 16 June 1970.

[3] For general information on temples in South India, see *Temples in South India*, Publications Division, Government of India, 1960, and R.K. Das, *Temples of Tamilnadu*, Bharatiya Vidya Bhavan, Bombay, 1964.

[4] For a general comment on this, see J. Adams and Uwe J. Woltemade, "Village Economy in Traditional India," *op. cit.*, pp. 52-53. See also M.N. Srinivas, *Religion and Society Among the Coorgs of South India, op. cit.*

[5] See M.N. Srinivas, *ibid.*, p. 26, and K. William Kapp, *Hindu Culture, Economic Development and Economic Planning in India*, Asia Publishing House, Bombay, 1963, pp. 21-40.

[6] M. Marriott "Little Communities in an Indigenous Civilization," in M. Marriott (ed.), *Village India*, University of Chicago Press, Chicago, 1955, p. 218.

[7] See Milton Singer, "The Social Organization of Indian Civilization," *op. cit.*

[8] This perspective is thoroughly developed in Max Weber, *The Religion of India*, The Free Press, Glencoe, 1958; M.N. Srinivas, *Cast in Modern India and Other Essays*, Asia Publishing House, Madras, 1962; and J.B. Pratt, *India and its Faiths*, Houghton Mifflin Company, Boston, 1915.

[9] The best treatment of this question, in general, is R. Hardgrave, Jr., *The Dravidian Movement, op. cit.* See also the other DMK referenc es cited in the notes of Chapter Six.

[10] For perspectives on this see Stephen Neill, *Christian Faith and Other Faiths*, Oxford University Press, London, 1961, Chapter 4; P.D. Devanandan, *The Gospel and Renascent Hinduism*, S.C.M. Press, London, 1959; and the *Religion and Society* issues (published under the auspices of the Christian Institute for the Study of Religion and Society, 19 Miller Road, Bangalore), XII, March 1965, and VIII, December 1961.

[11] At least twenty-one temples in Madras today have a yearly revenue of more than Rs 20,000 compared with fewer than fifteen, ten years ago. And, for example, the Palani temple, one of the most important pilgrimage centres in Madurai District, now has an income considerably more than forty lakh rupees a year compared with an income of only ten lakh rupees a decade ago. This information was obtained in an interview with the Deputy Director of the Hindu Religious Endowment Board, Madras, on 16 June 1970.

[12] On this, see general comments by Milton Singer, "The Radha Krishna Bhajans of Madras City," in *History of Religion*, 2 (Winter), 1963, and "The Social Organization of Indian Civilization," *op. cit.* Travelling minstrel programmes, group singing programmes, etc., often involve persons from many socio-economic backgrounds.

[13] Cf. Agehananda Bharati, "Hinduism and Modernization," *op.cit.*

[14] Interesting and informative on this matter is the series of articles that appeared in the journal, *The International Review of Missions*. See the articles by K. Baago, LV (July 1966), pp. 322-332; I.H. Douglas and J.B. Carman, LV (October 1966), pp. 483-489; K. Baago, LV (January 1967), pp. 99-103.

[15] For a history of the Christian Church in India, see C.B. Firth, *An Introduction to Indian Church History*, The Christian Literature Society, Madras, 1961.

[16] My "Protestant Missions in India: A Sociological Review," in *Journal of Asian and African Studies*, 5, October 1970, is a general statement on these kinds of considerations. See also my "Christianity and Social Change in South India," in *Practical Anthropology*, 17, May-June 1970. Personal research on the organization of the Church in Madras indicates understandings of the kind developed in these articles also can be used in understanding the Madras Church.

[17] In relation to an emerging dialogue between east and west, see the materials identified in footnote 10 above. See also S. Radhakrishnan, *Eastern Religions and Western Thought*, Oxford University Press, New York, 1959, and *East and West in Religion*, George Allen and Unwin, London, 1954.

[18] For general information on gods and goddesses in South India, see H. Whitehead, *Gods and Goddesses of South India*, Oxford University Press, 1921, and W.T. Elmore, *Dravidian Gods in Modern Hinduism*, Christian Literature Society Press, Madras, 1925. Refer also to relevant sections in some of the village studies identified, especially those in P.G. Hiebert, *Konduru: Structure and Integration in a South Indian Village*, *op. cit.*

[19] On this see John J. Gumperz, "Religion and Social Communication in Village North India," in Edward B. Harper (ed.), *Religion in South India*, University of Washington Press, Seattle, 1964.

[20] This temple was constructed about fifty years ago and was visited by Mahatma Gandhi in 1932. It today attracts fairly large crowds at festival times. Its economic needs, and those of the extended family that owns it, are provided for in relation to the rents taken in from the homes built on the lands of the temple.

[21] Life-cycle ceremonies in certain South Indian areas are described in a meaningful way in S.C. Dube, *Indian Village*, *op. cit.*, and M.N. Srinivas, *Religion and Society Among the Coorgs of South India*, *op. cit.*, pp. 70-123.

[22] Though this observation is true in general, especially for more westernized groups, it does not uniformly hold true for all groups, especially certain Vaisya level groups where there is a strong interest in retaining older patterns of behaviour. See G.N. Ramu, "Family and Kinship in Urban South India," *op. cit.*

[23] Paul D. Wiebe, "Small Town in Modern India," *op. cit.*, pp. 164-166.

Chapter 8

Schooling and Family Planning

SCHOOLING

Aspects of the General Context

As for India in general, Madras and Tamilnadu have made very impressive strides in the elimination of illiteracy, in the provision of educational facilities at the primary, middle, secondary, and university levels, and in the provision for various professional, technical, and adult-literacy programmes. In 1960-61, the Tamilnadu Government spent Rs 5.5 per capita on education; in 1965-66, Rs 10.5; in 1969-70, Rs 16.9. Already 94.1 per cent of the children in the 6-11 year-old age group are enrolled in schools, and by 1975 it is projected that 100 per cent of the children in this age category will be so enrolled.[1] The assumptions by the Tamilnadu Government, like those of the Government of India, have been that ". . .education plays a catalytic role in socio-economic development. . . [and] that education is a great factor in raising the productivity of the worker in any sector of [the] economy."[2]

Changes in the concepts and organization of education in Tamilnadu have had many manifestly positive results. Whereas certain groups of people within the Indian system of social organization once had much greater access to an education than did others, by now an access to a basic education is officially considered the right of every child. And thus new avenues of socio-economic mobility have been opened up for groups formerly disadvantaged and such avenues are continuously becoming better defined.

At the same time, however, changes in the organization of education have led to certain problematic consequences. For one thing, the problem of employment for the educated is becoming increasingly severe. A feature article in the *Hindu* phrased the problem thus:

> The tremendous rush for admission to the Pre-University Course
> in college provokes the question: What do these boys and girls,
> the bright ones and the not so bright ones, hope to accomplish?
> Do they have a plan, goal, something they are determined to achieve?
> For most it seems entry into college is a stepping stone on the road
> to some future employment, an inevitable necessity in the world of
> competition and as one of them tersely put it: What is the
> chance for SSLCs (Secondary School Leaving Certificate holders)
> when graduates compete for posts of bus conductors, police
> constables and peons?[3]

A member of the Tamilnadu Assembly in a speech before the House
called the current employment possibilities of teachers in the state
"appalling."[4] R.A. Gopalswamy, former Director of the Institute of
Applied Manpower Planning, recognizing the shortages of job
opportunities and the under-emphasis on practical training in the
state's schools, claimed the pressure on the education system was
such that there is little possibility of linking education to employment
under the present system.[5] In that economic growth patterns have
not kept up with those postulated, the unemployment of engineers
has become a problem in Tamilnadu and in India.[6] The problem of
finding employment suitable to relatively lower levels of education,
meanwhile, remains even more severe.

A second problem relates to the pressures for admission to higher
level educational institutions. Given the emphasis on education for
all and the problems of employment, in recent years the rush for
admission has resulted in a number of malpractices. For example,
admission to many institutions, especially private institutions and the
better institutions, is now often correlated with the willingness to
make financial donations to particular projects or the ability to use
effectively the influences one is in a position to bring to bear on administrators and admissions personnel.[7] In consequence, the best educa-
tions are often almost exclusively available only to the more
advantaged in society.

A third problem is that along with the increase in the number of
children educated there has often also been a decline in the quality
of public education, and remarks to this effect are common in Madras.[8]

Finally, the problem of inadequate facilities persists. In Madras

seen against the space standards (defined as acceptable) most of the schools within the city are sub-standard with 69 per cent of Primary and Middle Schools and 48 per cent of High Schools not having any playgrounds at all, while 28 per cent in the former and 45.7 per cent in the latter have some but not adequate playground facilities. Only 3 per cent of the Primary Schools and 6 per cent of the High Schools come up to the norms fixed for playgrounds. The situation is similar as regards class room space also. Many of the buildings for schools particularly primary and middle are *kutcha*, lacking in essential facilities, and a sizeable number of them are in rented buildings. Some idea of these conditions can be gathered from the fact that more than 30 per cent of the 349 Corporation Primary Schools are in rented buildings. 25 per cent of the 435 Primary and Secondary Schools run by the City Corporation are in *kutcha* buildings. Almost all schools have inadequate lavatory and water facilities and teaching equipment.[9]

The problems related to the development of education in Tamilnadu and Madras are serious. Yet the official emphasis on this development continues. Furthermore, this emphasis is clearly supported in the continued clamour of the people for more educational facilities and services. Most of the people who seek secure employment positions consider education a "must" in terms of the context in which they live.

Schooling in Chennanagar

Illiteracy rates in Chennanagar are relatively lower for the younger than for older people. Whereas 74 per cent of the women and 40 per cent of the men over thirty are illiterate, only 50 per cent of the women and 20 per cent of the men between the ages of ten and thirty are illiterate (see Table 3.2). Furthermore, it is reasonable to assume that even greater proportions of the young will become literate in the course of time. A certain embarassment today accompanies illiteracy, especially among males, and schools are now more accessible to the Chennanagar young than they ever were to most of their elders. Education has certainly made inroads into the lives of the people.

Nevertheless, the problems associated with education in the Madras context also limit the educational process in Chennanagar. The primary school the Chennanagar children attend is situated about a mile and a half away, in another slum area. The two buildings involved are small (about 15' by 30') and thatch-roofed, with cane lattice work between the roof and the masonry walls. The concrete floors are pitted. Neither building shelters well against the rains.

According to the ward councillor, the education offered in this and the other three corporation schools in the ward is very poor. His explanation here puts the blame on the teachers, the children, and the parents:

> The teachers are not interested in teaching. Even though they have security in their positions and get good salaries, they are lazy and more interested in themselves than in teaching. I could get some of them transfered to other places, but what good would that do? We would probably get worse teachers in their place. The children are not interested in their studies and parents neglect encouraging their children to attend school. My son is an example here. He is in the fourth standard but he does not yet even know how to read the alphabet well. He doesn't like school.

The facilities available to the children are negligible. Except for blackboards there is nothing. The children bring their own slates, writing materials, and notebooks to school. Teacher-pupil learning occurs along the lines of memorization and repetition in unison.

In reality, only ten to fifteen children attend the corporation school on most days. The remainder stay in the *nagar* or wander around in the neighbourhood. The largest Chennanagar *manram* once offered a night class in reading and writing, the second DMK *manram* still irregularly offers one. But the first discontinued its classes because of very poor attendance and the lack of teaching personnel, and the second, when it does offer a class, seldom finds more than four or five children in attendance.

One adult male gives private instruction in reading and writing about every other morning for an hour, at a rate of 50 n.p. per month per child. He commonly has about fifteen young children in attendance. His group meets under a tree, sometimes learning with enthusiasm but more often representing as much a supervised play period as a class situation. Only five or six young people attend high school.

The problems the Chennanagar children have in securing a good formal education are obvious; and just as obviously, few of them succeed in this. Yet the notion that education is a means whereby better (more secure, better paid, and more regular) occupational positions can be achieved is well developed among the people. Though very few of the families would think of trying to educate equally all their children, almost all would like to see at least one of their sons with at least a high school education, and most would like their daughters to get at least an eighth or a ninth standard education. As one of our informants put it: "With an SSLC, almost anyone can find a job for there are so many industries coming up nowadays. Most of these industries want employees who have at least a high-school education." Another said: "My daughter should be educated up to the eighth standard and should pick up some trade such as sewing. Then if her husband is not able to provide she will be able to help."

The general feeling is that an education helps a person find an occupation other than those usually associated with slum people. Ironically, however — and no matter how true this is for some of the people — with the tightening up of the job market, even for the better educated, the people here have come to adopt this feeling firmly even at a time when it is no longer as valid as it once was.

FAMILY PLANNING

Consciously correlating many of their economic and developmental problems with their rapid growth in population, Indians since Independence have dramatically developed family planning emphases. On the one hand, they have quite regularly and routinely increased (at least until recently) the financial allotments to family planning programmes. On the other, they have increasingly diversified the techniques used in the dissemination of family planning information and they have increasingly recognized and resolved the problems associated with the communication of family planning ideas. The amount allotted in the First Five Year Plan was Rs 6.5 million; in the Second and Third Plans, it went up to Rs 50 million and Rs 62.12 million respectively. In the Fourth Plan, the amount allotted was Rs 900 million.[10] Though it is overwhelmingly clear that much remains to be done, remarkable progress in family planning has been made in India.[11]

In Tamilnadu, the government has been exceptionally active in popularizing family planning. Radio broadcasts, newspaper advertisements, special public occasions, and other mass media forms present the message in all parts of the state. And by now, the red triangle symbol and the sketch of the family of adequate size — husband, wife, and two children — are widely recognized by the people as government backed propaganda indications of the need for family planning. In addition to the more than 100 family planning clinics in Tamilnadu, today there are more than 122 primary health centres in which family planning work is done, twelve district hospitals where sterilizations are performed and 108 *taluk* hospitals where minor surgeries related to the planning of families are performed.[12]

In Madras, the programme of family planning is organized around a District Family Planning Bureau and its subsidiary twenty-four Urban Family Welfare Planning Centres. Each Centre coordinates family planning activities in an area of the city. This area, in turn, is subdivided into four sectors, and each sector into ten blocks each consisting of about 200-250 eligible couples. Family planning personnel in each area "...impart sound knowledge about the family planning methods and precisely preach the small family norms."[13] They also "serve" willing couples in supplementary ways. In relation to the chains of service the Madras family planning service has organized, it estimates that it has "...succeeded in increasing the number of eligible couples following Family Planning from a previous 6 per cent [a figure arrived at shortly after the organization of family planning, above outlined, was initiated on 10 February 1967] to 38.1 per cent in April 1970."[14]

Considering the problems of determining such percentage figures, under any circumstances, and the problems associated with the appreciation of figures provided by a city agency trying to meet certain quota goals, the figures just given should be viewed with some skepticism. Nevertheless, taken together with the tremendous mobilization of effort, such figures do indicate that strides are being made in the directions desired.

Family Planning in the Slums of Madras

As a part of a general study of social welfare in the slums of Madras, the Madras School of Social Work sought answers to the following questions: How aware of family planning are slum dwellers? How many practice family planning? Are they interested in learning about it? What are their objections to family planning? The School's answers to these questions were developed on the basis of sample survey materials collected in 1964.[15]

The following are some answers: (*i*) whereas 55.1 per cent of the respondents had some knowledge of family planning, only 4.6 per cent practiced family planning; (*ii*) among the 44.9 per cent who did not know about family planning, 85.82 per cent said they had no interest in learning about family planning; (*iii*) only 40.8 per cent of the respondents were aware of some of the specific techniques involved in family planning; (*iv*) the most well-known technique — "probably due more to propaganda and the economic rewards accompanying sterilization" — was sterilization (a technique known by 36.2 per cent of the sample); (*v*) the principal argument against family planning (an argument given by 38.67 per cent of those who had heard of family planning but were not practicing it) was "...just because of dislike," other reasons were because it is unnecessary (27.62 per cent), bad for health (11.05 per cent), because family planning techniques are ineffective (9.12 per cent), because family planning violates religious understandings (6.62 per cent) and so on (6.92 per cent); and (*vi*) the more educated and the economically better off among the respondents seem to be more likely to practice family planning than the others.

Since the time of the Madras School of Social Work study, many changes in family planning in Madras have taken place. The Health Officer for family planning in the district describes the current situation as follows:

Of the 65,210 eligible slum couples (a figure determined in early 1970), 11,482 have accepted some FP method. The District Family Planning Bureau has organized intense motivation drives for loop and sterilization in the slums where the need for FP is felt more when compared to other areas. The concentrated efforts of the staff have given fruitful results. About 2,100 mothers have been inserted with loop. Nearly 1,300 men have undergone vasectomy and 700 women have undergone tubectomy. More than 6,900 are using some conventional contraceptives. Nearly 50 persons are using oral pill as a method of contraception.

The leaders in the slums have been contacted regularly and frequently for their cooperation in motivating the eligible couples in their area. Special orientation camps have been organized for them to make them participate in the FP Programmes. The Youth Organizations, Welfare Centres, Political Clubs and Sangams have been contacted to enlist the cooperation of the members in the motivation camps organized by FP Staff.

Due to all efforts, the percentage of acceptance of FP which was 12.6 per cent on March 31, 1969 has been raised to 17.6 per cent on March 31, 1970. With intensified education and motivation the District Family Planning Bureau will surely strive to increase the FP acceptance in the years to come.[16]

Meanwhile, the obstacles in the way of further acceptance of family planning methods and emphases are the kinds of things above mentioned in relation to the review of the Madras School of Social Work study.

Family Planning in Chennanagar

To help define family planning usages and attitudes in Chennanagar, quota samples of twenty-two married women and twenty-one married men, all with children in their homes or still of a child-bearing age, were selected. Member individuals were then asked a few relevant questions in a situation giving each as much privacy as possible. Findings from this little sub-study are now presented.

Table 8.1

NUMBER OF CHILDREN IN FAMILIES OF RESPONDENTS
IN FAMILY PLANNING STUDY

Number of children in family	Male respondents	Female respondents
0	5	2
1—2	1	4
3—4	10	8
5—6	4	8
6+	1	—

First, it is clear that the people formally acknowledge that the family size should be restricted. Table 8.1 shows the number of children in the families investigated. Table 8.2 shows the number the respondents considered optimal. A comparison of these tables shows the "optimal numbers" to be lower in distribution than is the case for the others. Furthermore, though the number of respondents who consider as optimal the government encouraged number of 1-2 children is less than the number of those who would prefer 3-4 children, the "optimal number" distribution obviously is more weighted in the desired direction than is the other distribution. Only two women respondents formally hold the view that the number of children that come along is the best number.

Table 8.2

NUMBER OF CHILDREN CONSIDERED OPTIMAL BY RESPONDENTS IN FAMILY PLANNING STUDY

Optimal number of children	Male respondents	Female respondents
1—2	7	5
3—4	13	15
5—6	1	—
Any number	—	2

Second, almost all the people are aware of at least one way in which to prevent the conception of children and most of them are aware of several ways. Table 8.3 presents relevant distributions.

All but one of the women and sixteen of the twenty-one men respondents said they knew of sterilization as a family planning procedure. Sixteen women and eleven men said they knew of the use of birth control pills. Other standard contraceptive procedures were known by fewer people.

Third, with regard to the practice of contraception, little had occurred. One woman had tried to use a local technique but this had not worked and she had conceived anyway. Fourteen women had never tried to practice contraception and expressed no interest in doing so. Of the other seven women respondents, three claimed

Table 8.3

AWARENESS OF FAMILY PLANNING TECHNIQUES AMONG RESPONDENTS
IN FAMILY PLANNING STUDY

Number of techniques known	Male respondents	Female respondents
1—2	6	3
3—4	9	11
5+	4	7
Don't know	2	1

they wanted to be sterilized, four that they wanted to start taking pills. For the male respondents, one said he was sterilized, one that he used condoms, and one that his wife had been sterilized. Of the other eighteen, sixteen did not show any interest in family planning and two did not answer the question involved. In sum, with respect to the forty-three married couples for whom information is presented here, only four (9.4 per cent) were using any technique of contraception in their homes.

The principal reasons given for not practicing family planning included the opinions that family planning would reduce a person's productivity and lead to weakness and poor health. Other reasons concerned problems associated with the lack of privacy and poor sanitary conditions. Contrariwise, to explain why many people were now thinking more seriously of family planning, most people used reasons pertaining to their own economic and employment scarcities. None of the people gave only one-sided answers to explain their perspectives; all expressed mixed motivations. Thirty-two of the forty-three respondents favoured their government's attempts to control the growth of population.

REFERENCES

[1] These and other relevant materials can be found in the Finance Department, Government of Tamilnadu publication, *Tamil Nadu: An Economic Appraisal, 1971-1972*, Madras, 1971, pp. 70-75.

[2] *Ibid.*, p. 70.

[3] The *Hindu*, 27 January 1971.

[4] Reported in the *Hindu*, 25 June 1971.

[5] Reported in the *Sunday Standard*, 27 June 1971.

[6] A news article in the *Hindu*, 18 May 1970, estimated that 100,000 engineers in India would be unemployed by the end of the Fourth Plan in 1973-74.

[7] For more information on this point, see the *Hindu* articles, "Minister's Defence of Tamil Medium," and "Donations for Seats: Colleges Warned," in the issues of 11 July 1971 and 19 July 1970, respectively. For a more thorough perspective of the entire problem, see G.N. Ramu, "Family and Kinship in Urban South India," *op. cit.*, especially Chapters 7 and 8.

[8] For comparative comments on this see the *Hindu* article, 27 June 1971, "Where Do They Go from Here?" See also the *Indian Express* article, 10 July 1971, "Every Child Will be in School by 1975."

[9] Tamilnadu Directorate of Town Planning, *Interim Plan: Madras Metropolitan Area*, *op. cit.*, pp. 110-111.

[10] Reported in G.N. Ramu, "Factors that Retard Family Planning Movement," in *Family Planning News*, June 1968, p. 16.

[11] For general information on family planning, the problems associated with population growth in India, and trends and projections, see K.K. Dewett, G.C. Singh, and J.D. Varma, *Indian Economics*, S. Chand and Co Ltd., Delhi, 1971, pp. 69-95.

[12] These figures are contained in the Madras School of Social Work study, *Social Welfare in the Slums of Madras*, New India Publishers, Madras, 1965.

[13] Corporation of Madras mimeographed circular, "District Family Planning Bureau on the Pathway to Progress," prepared about the middle of 1970, p. 2.

[14] *Ibid.*, p. 6.

[15] The sample (N = 1,000) consisted of heads of families randomly selected from approximately 10 per cent of the city's slums. A questionnaire developed for the purposes of the study, and pre-tested, was used to gather the materials reported. For the materials covered in this paragraph, see the Madras School of Social Work study, *op. cit.*, pp. 63-74.

[16] "Family Planning Work in Slums," a report prepared for us by the Health Officer, Madras District Family Planning Bureau, July 1970.

Nine

Conclusions

Many pictures of life in Chennanagar remain which are not given in the materials presented. I remember sitting in their coffee shops and drinking coffee at their expense, in turn buying cups of coffee for many of them. I often listened to their explanations of what they do and what they would like to do while watching them smoke their *beedis*, work their shuttles, and stitch their clothing. I remember eating happily offered *idlis* with delicious *sambar* (a spicy onion sauce) off plates very minimally cleaned, with flies landing all around. I recall a rather saucy Muslim woman, neatly dressed for a trip down town, splattered with mud as she walked because she offended certain local sensitivities. A little old woman once came with a *barre* (a female water-buffalo) she greatly prized and wanted to be photographed alongside. I had the experience of being charged by an angry *barre* while idling on a motor scooter, and coming within ten feet of having the beast on top of me — my hasty retreat to the hilarious enjoyment of those with whom I had been chatting.

I remember a family carefully dressing up a dying elder of theirs who they wanted thus photographed. I remember a mother of six little boys with five of her little ones nakedly sitting around her, receiving their tiny portions of food, while the sixth, tied to a wooden post outside the hut, in punishment, screamed his protest.

I remember also the sensual pleasure of a long cold shower in my Indian hotel room after a period in Chennanagar, a pleasure mixed with a certain feeling of guilt as I remembered the scarcity of water, and the need for it in the place from which I had just returned.

Life goes on in many of its routine, fascinating, and peculiar ways in a place like Chennanagar. And many more perspectives would be possible.

However, of course, all such perspectives cannot be treated in a study such as this. What's more, considering its purposes, this study is now relatively complete. Concluding, then, we remain with the kinds of questions raised in Chapter One. And to these we shall now return. Do "culture of poverty" kinds of delineations apply in the understanding of social life in Chennanagar? And how does our view "from the bottom" enable us to answer the questions involved in what in Chapter One we labelled the biased, negative approaches used by many in their discussions of slum life in India? Following our discussion of the answers to these two questions, we shall seek a tentative answer to the general question: Why does poverty in certain social contexts tend to breed social pathologies whereas in others it does not? We shall then conclude with a brief review of some of the implications our understandings have for planning considerations.

POVERTY WITHOUT A "CULTURE OF POVERTY"

To review, in general, the kinds of outlines appropriately drawn in Chapter One (and associated there, primarily and quite rightly with the work of Oscar Lewis), if people live in a "culture of poverty" (i) there will locally be a minimum of social organization beyond the nuclear and extended family and the situation will locally represent an anomalous and marginal pattern of organization in an otherwise organized society; (ii) there will be a disengagement of local life from the society's major institutions and the development of alternative institutions; (iii) childhood here will not be specially prolonged, initiation into sex comes early, the family tends to become mother-centred and the head of the family is given to authoritarian rule; and (iv) the individual, under such conditions, will have strong feelings of fatalism, dependence, helplessness and so on.

The people of Chennanagar definitely live in conditions of poverty and the handicaps they know in many ways are severely limiting. But do they live in a "culture of poverty?"

Organization of Local Social Life

Chennanagar is not simply an aggregate of disorganized peoples. Reviewing the local organization of the family first, family living is prevalent. Some of the men have concubines or mistresses in other places and most people see a certain breakdown in extended and joint family patterns of living. Almost all the local people, however, live in households with their spouses and children. And many have living with them other members of their more extended kin networks. In many families, the members work together in household kinds of industries. In most families, marriage partners are selected for individuals with the help of parents and other family elders, or selected go-betweens, and many ceremonies of the religious and life-cycle calendars are observed by individuals as members in their family units. In general, children are carefully cared for and many are encouraged to seek occupations that will enable them to live some day in better circumstances than those that Chennanagar affords. The conditions of life here have made it impossible for most people to retain, in good order, some of their more extended kinship relationships. In their conditions of scarcity, the people in many ways have been forced to fend for themselves in nuclear family units, and the difficulties they experience in terms of availing themselves of communication and transportation facilities, with their limited financial resources, further cut them off from some of the more thorough associations they once may have had with relatives in other places. But nuclear family living within the ideal conceptualization that more extended family living would be nice, remains an important fact of life here.

Second, and in immediate consequence to the above, though family ties in Chennanagar do not tie so directly into caste networks as they do in many more traditionally defined settings in India, almost all marriages continue to be arranged within caste lines. The problems confronted by the local people of inter-caste marriages — let alone those these people foresee for their children — speak for this. So do such things as the fact that the people know their caste identities and the importance of caste in their general context. In reference to the latter, at least implicitly, they know of the operations of caste factors in such things as employment, promotions, and politics.

Within Chennanagar, caste considerations remain important in relation to personal and family kinds of identifications, much less so and sometimes not at all in relation to occupations, dress codes, household arrangement patterns and so on. Indeed, almost no differences among the people of different castes remain, considering the latter. But again, in the ways caste identifications continue to operate in the local setting and in the larger society, they remain important in the organization of local life.

Third, our evidence points clearly to a high degree of political organization in Chennanagar. In fact, an alignment with one or another of the local *manrams* is essential for all the people. *Manram* leaders control the local distribution of water and they were instrumental in bringing the various supplies of water to the *nagar* in the first place.

Manrams are the platforms in relation to which local leaders emerge and it is through these leaders that local people are often represented to outsiders. Recreational facilities — for example, carrom boards — too expensive for local households to own individually, are accessible to those who are eligible to use them, at the *manrams*. It is under the cover of the leading Chennanagar *manram* that the Madras Christian Council of Social Service and other agencies locally distribute their welfare items, and it is through their own *manram* leaders that people who do not belong to the first *manram* often express their dissatisfaction with such procedures. The members of the *nagar's* first *manram* tore down the temporary building the members of the second *manram* erected when they did so on lands set aside for other purposes.

The caste unit has often been found important in the organization of activities and interests in more traditionally organized areas in India. In Chennanagar, caste remains important but the situation here is not as it is in more traditional settings. Importantly, in short, activities and interests here are more and more coming to be organized in relation to entities that can get things done for their members. Through their *manrams*, the people have been able to do things for themselves: through these organizations they have been able to coordinate their requests and, at times, demands, for outside assistance.

Finally, at least for these review purposes, it is becoming increasingly clear that Chennanagar will more and more become a community in its own right. Chennanagar's geographical outlines are clear; sales people have come to identify this community as their own sales area; local people have set up their own shops and tea stalls and local shop owners gain most of their clientele from the Chennanagar people. The people here have their own temple and they celebrate certain festivals together. Whatever conflicts do occur locally, almost all the people by now have invested what are to them considerable sums of money in their households. And they have come to see how these investments will pay off, in the long run, in economic and other terms.

Chennanagar's original settlement occurred without legal permission but, at least for the foreseeable future, this community will persist.

And within this community the people will continue to organize themselves, in ways holding on to some of the traditional structural supports with which they are provided by their civilization, in others adjusting older with newer forms in getting things done.

Interrelationships Between Chennanagar and its Environments

Turning next to the question of the interrelationships between Chennanagar and its various environments, we find it impossible to think of Chennanagar as a community cut off in any significant cultural or social ways. First, religious attitudes and behaviours tie the people into their more general contexts. The Chennanagar temple is important in local religious life in the ways we have specified, but so are the many other temples and pilgrimage centres with which the people are associated and which they visit when they can and will. None of the people think of their religious systems as locally circumscribed, and even the charms and amulets that are considered helpful are defined by them in terms of the understandings they have gained from itinerent holy men or in their visits to local or other religious places.

Economically, meanwhile, it is obvious that Chennanagar's patterns cannot be understood apart from those of the city. The person who locally sells kerosene at a profit of 1 n.p. a litre buys it in bulk from a wholesaler. The old woman who sweeps out three homes in a nearby residential area at an agreed monthly rate, in turn subletting the rights to sweep one of these houses to another woman, conducts her business in terms of the opportunities she knows in the city. A family, eligible for corporation sponsored housing, chooses instead to live in Chennanagar, gaining an income by renting its reserved corporation quarters to another family. And so on.

Conditions of unemployment and underemployment in the context undoubtedly affect the capacities of the people to provide for their own living securities. But they have found many ways of earning a little money within the Madras setting. On the one hand, they thus provide for themselves and their dependents, on the other, they work as integral parts in the Madras labour force. It is impossible to think of the city's economic activities going on without the participation of people like those who live in Chennanagar.

In reference to political ties out of Chennanagar, the capacities of the Chennanagar people to get things done for them are intricately related to the developments that have been occurring in modern, democratic India. Given the vote, the people have been put in a position where they can demand the services of politicians, in return for their support, and they have.

We have seen how an understanding of DMK political successes in Tamilnadu must be related to an understanding of the successful mobilization of lower class political support and we have seen how this support has been offered and accepted in relation to the Chennanagar setting. The allowance to settle the dump area that became Chennanagar was given by DMK politicians. So were such things as the supply of water, the definitions of local tenure rights and so on. Similarly, for example, the Chennanagar Congress *manram* members, through their leaders now seek to get a local water supply in return for their support of the Congress area councillor and what he can do for them.

The political ties between area-wide political leaders and the Chennanagar people, thus identifiable, in ways are understandable in terms of the paternalistic patterns of authority that long have characterized the relationships between "higher" and "lower" levels of people in the Indian system of social stratification. At the same time, however, they are the very stuff of modern, democratic processes. As the earlier Congress administration in Tamilnadu became encrusted by the interests of political bosses and divorced from the interests of the common people, the DMK came to realize its support among many of the poor people and, eventually, to gain political power in the state as well as the city.

The Chennanagar people early found support in the DMK, and at the time of this study, the majority of them still strongly support this party: the main *manram* had as its president the Labour Minister of Tamilnadu, the second, a locally important DMK lawyer. But meaningful for the people as the support of the DMK has been, this does not mean such support will necessarily persist. Necessary "pay-offs" are built into the relationship that occurs but our evidence points to the fact the ties will wither should the persons outside, in a position to help the Chennanagar people, lose their interest in helping. Again, the Chennanagar people can do much for themselves, and they do. Also, however, they need the help of important outsiders, for their own capacities are limited. Regarding the latter, it appears that they have come to understand the ways in which they can use their votes to gain the attention they need.

In short, the channels of modern political relationships extend into Chennanagar and the Chennanagar people have come to use these whether or not they understand some of the more abstract meanings and ideologies of the term "democracy."

Many other ways in which the relationships between Chennanagar and its more general contexts occur could be outlined. The cinema is locally popular especially among the younger men, and the leading actors and actresses can be identified by many of the people. Transportation and communication networks link Chennanagar with all the other parts of the city. Officials, family planning personnel, census ennumerators, and others with ideas and items too numerous to mention come into Chennanagar or influence the people as they move about in various parts of the city. At least some of the people approach police officers and court officials for particular purposes.

But enough has already been given in review to allow for an understanding of the ways in which the social life of Chennanagar is tied in with that of its various environments.

Local Family Life

We have already reviewed some of the characteristics of family living in Chennanagar stating that here kinship relationships beyond the nuclear family have been cut off to a considerable extent. Additionally, there is little opportunity in Chennanagar for privacy within the family context — the huts are small, with no interior walls in most of them — and there is an early initiation into sex.

But again, such characteristics, though they do fit the general model of the "culture of poverty," do not fit together here, with other features, to result in the same. For example, we find no indication in Chennanagar of a developing mother-centred authoritarianism within the family setting, and little if any indication that basic, preferential processes of mate selection are being revised.

Simultaneously we have found that a high regard for children persists. Some of the local parents have lost contact with certain of their children; quite a few feel their older and married children, now living in other places, have lost interest in them. The ties with their children that do remain for most parents, however, and the interests these parents repeatedly express in such things as the welfare, educational opportunities, employment, and "returns" their children may some day provide for them speak for the interests of these parents in continuing their families' welfare. The Chennanagar people know of their "native places," of their identities within the Indian configuration of caste, and the rules they must follow in contracting marriages.

The Individual

Our interest in this study has not been in the individual attributes, values, and character structure of the people and, thus, we cannot deal appropriately with the fourth general dimension in the conceptualization of the "culture of poverty," as this can be applied to Chennanagar. In passing, though, it seems likely that here too our understandings of this community's social life would lead us to reject the idea that the local people live in such a culture. This is the case as the attitudes and values of these people are clearly not locally circumscribed in any way, they are not describable as hopeless or helpless, they are not geared only to immediate gratification and they are identifiable with desires for improvements and change. The people, in illustration, know how to approach outsiders for assistance. They also know how to bribe others in attempting to gain advantages and they do so when necessary And they plan for their own welfare and the welfare of those in their households.

A Conclusion

It is not certain all of the preconditions for the emergence of a "culture of poverty" occur in Madras. The city is "modern" and industrial in many ways, yet it does not resemble the kinds of cities in western capitalistic societies where some of the poor are most likely to develop a "culture of poverty" as an "...adaptation and a reaction ...to their marginal position."[1]

Given such questions as this might imply, however, it seems abundantly clear a "culture of poverty" does not now characterize the living patterns of the Chennanagar people and that such a culture does not now seem to be emerging. The "old" and the "new" in conjunction with each other are producing various new forms of social life in Chennanagar. But it is not possible to delineate fully any of the local patterns that occur without reference to similar or related patterns in the Madras, Tamilnadu, and Indian environments.

CORRECTING SOME MISINTERPRETATIONS

Looking from the "bottom:" Are the Chennanagar people victims only of their environment, unable to help themselves? Are they unable to "function properly?" Are they "unsocialized?" Are they peculiar in the ways in which they define their goals and seek to achieve them? Is there no "hope" among them? Have they no ability to define leadership among themselves? Is the community only a "cancerous growth" on the body social of Madras? On the basis of our data our answers to all these and similar questions have to be negative. Looking at social life in Madras at the "bottom," from the perspectives of the people themselves, we find the kinds of evaluations thus far commonly available in the literatures on slum living in India to be widely erroneous both for an understanding of Chennanagar life and, by implication, for an understanding of slum life in other such contexts.

LOOKING AT POVERTY IN ITS INDIAN CONTEXT

Many reasons for why the Chennanagar people do not live in a "culture of poverty" can be given. Oscar Lewis,[2] finding no such culture in India in his studies — none of which were conducted in places like Madras and Bombay where, according to his own specifications, the culture in India would most likely be expected, but anyway—identifies some of these.[2] Some of the same, and others, we now can identify in relation to our own understandings of social life in Chennanagar. These include the following: the influence of caste and family organization in India; indigenous religious beliefs and practices; emergent political processes; attitudes towards education; local emphases in urban planning, and slum clearance and development; and the underlying reasons for optimism that locally exist.

In general, social life in Chennanagar can be fully understood only in relation to the continuities of Indian civilization. These occur despite, or perhaps better because of, the compartmentalization process that began to emerge in antiquity and continue today. These have seen develop an organic unity among the society's different social units (castes and caste-like entities) within an encompassing ideological system. More specifically, structures (as we have seen) that still thoroughly influence the organization of social life in Madras and the other cities of Tamilnadu and India, while also influencing life in the villages of the area and the country. . .these structures also help pattern the ways in which the Chennanagar people relate themselves to each other.

Concurrently, India's ideological system allows for a tremendous diversity within its embrasive reach. Thus, for example, it recognizes the relevance of both the magical-animistic and the highly abstract among its followers, always encouraging "higher" levels of beliefs and practices — through its various systems as these may be represented in the teachings of priests and prophets, the central importance of regional temples and pilgrimage centres, and so on — but at the same time never categorically shutting out of its compass those who might consider themselves members of other ideological systems. The Chennanagar people find for their religious procedures supports and clarifications in the teachings of those in their environment who "know more" than they do. And the people know of the larger temples and pilgrimage centres around and of outsiders who can teach them.

Chennanagar's Muslims and Christians, when compared with the community's Hindus, fare somewhat differently. But the Muslims in Madras, as in many other Indian contexts, retain their community solidarity and their ideological specificity, and the Chennanagar Muslims know of their ties with Muslims in other places. The Chennanagar Christians, meanwhile, generally belong to churches in other places, and these churches are linked with larger church and mission programmes.

Traditional features of Indian social and cultural life certainly can be related to an understanding of the social life of the people in Chennanagar and of the relations between these people and others. But so too can some of the modern patterns that India knows. And foremost here must be an understanding of the ways in which modern political processes have impinged on Chennanagar. It will undoubtedly remain clear that the mobilization of the lower classes will continue to play an important part in local and area-wide elections. And thus, so will the participation in these by people like those in Chennanagar.

Other factors that have led to the local organization of social life and links with the outside pertain to the recognized importance of education among the people and the increasing importance of planning and development activities. Whether or not there is a surplus of educated people in the area — and we have seen that there is — the Chennanagar people, of a social position that in the past were never encouraged, or even allowed to gain an education, now have this opportunity open to them, even forced upon them, in their early years.

The educational facilities of the area are grossly inadequate and the teaching is often ineffective. Yet the people see education as a means by which they can develop their understandings, compete more successfully for better jobs, find jobs with more security, and so on. In the words of one of our informants: "Without an education our children will grow up like we are, unable to talk well with officials." The implications are, of course, that education better enables such capacities and that these are important.

Meanwhile, programmes of slum clearance, slum development, and other assistance programmes sponsored by private and governmental agencies certainly have been geared for people like those in Chennanagar. And they know of them, though often only partially, or incorrectly, for such programmes can have much importance for them. Whether or not they eventually do, though, such programmes serve to link the people into their environments.

Then too, the "optimism" that comes, "... out of the understanding that any formal obstacle can be circumvented if one has the right patron or the right amount of money," buoys up the people. Indian society is characterized at least as much as most other societies, by gaps between the "haves" and the "have-nots," officialdom and those for whom official plans are described, the powerful and the weak. In rural areas, such gaps have resulted in the suspicion of outsiders and what they bear, on the part of villagers, and the latter have often hidden their perspectives behind masks of ignorance, their possessions behind "mud walls," in order to channel their contacts with the outsiders.[3] In urban India — especially in modern India with its emphases on social welfare programmes — it is similarly reasonable for many to mask their wealth and understandings when confronted by outsiders, until it is understood whether or not the contacts will be to the advantage of the persons involved in relation to the possibilities the outsiders represent.

In a place like Chennanagar, however, the "gaps" between the local people and possibly helpful outsiders can be bridged. In this connection, whether or not a particular success in establishing helpful associations with others will later result in another fruitful relationship, in the same manner, is not the problem. The fact of the possibility of doing so seems enough. Institutionalized in terms of both traditional and current reality is the feeling on the part of the people that given the right means of approach to a possibly helpful other, the approach can always be made.

Now, Chennanagar is not an old slum. Because of this, it might be possible to say it does not yet manifest social pathologies only because

these have not yet had the time to develop. On the basis of the knowledge gained of social processes in surrounding slums (some of which
are more than forty to fifty years old) and on the basis of what we have
found in Chennanagar, on the other hand, it appears that even with
much more time, "culture of poverty" kinds of pathologies will
not develop here.

Another Conclusion

It is possible that there is something like the "culture of poverty"
in various poor communities in the world, particularly in the
Caribbean. Indeed, however much they might be refuted (for example,
by scholars like C. Valentine), the contentions of people like Oscar
Lewis need to be further investigated. And they will be. In many
places it seems possible the local poor are so thoroughly cut off from
national forms of social organization and culture that they come to
feel isolated, distrustful of one another and so on.

In India, however, where political parties compete for the votes of
the poor and where both "old" and "new" traditional cultural forms
emphasize continuity across strata and classes, the poor may consider
themselves only as poor, not also as people outside the society and its
"shared rules of interpersonal decency."[4] At least such would be the
kinds of conclusions we would have to draw on the basis of our study.

Available to the Chennanagar people in the context of their civilization, are material and emotional resources that define their conditions of poverty, as stark as they are, in terms other than those that
would have to be used in describing conditions of poverty in, for
example, Latin American communities. The conditions of poverty
in India are such that they must be evaluated in their own terms.

SOME IMPLICATIONS

The problems of policies related to and programmes for slum clearance and development in India, as in many other parts of the world,
are complex and multi-faceted. Noting the power of the government
to do something about slum improvement and clearance, but the
uneven progress to date, P. Ramachandran comments :

> ...in fairness to the government...in trying to use its powers and
> develop its policies it has to take into account the low income of the
> people, the huge gap between income and shelter costs, land specu-

lation, lack of individual and national finance and savings, absence
of a well organized building industry, backwardness in architecture
and the use of local materials, public pressures, political influences,
influences in the selection of personnel and consequent inefficient
administration, corruption, etc.[5]

Noting such problems— problems also found in many other parts
of the world, of course, and certainly in both the so-called "affluent"
and "developing" countries — Ramachandran also says that in
addition to slum clearance and re-housing schemes it is essential
that "quick result yielding" schemes be encouraged.

What is required is a ...scheme which will help temporarily solve
the problem and yet provide the springboard for later permanent
solutions. Any such scheme must take into account two facts,
viz. that the resources at our disposal are extremely limited, and
that there is no point, when the problem is so gigantic, to talk in
terms of decent housing. What we should talk of is decent locality.
There is also no point in importing into the discussion standards
of privacy and spaciousness. The people living in these slums do
not have either of them now and they do not seem to be too keen
on having them either.[6]

Proceeding along similar lines, D.R. Gadgil urges that both short
and long-term goals must be developed and that the goals and procedures identified in India must be reflective of India's conditions of
life, not of those in other nations.[7]
In reference to the development of policies related to, and programmes for slum clearance and development, the Government of
India has long recognized the needs for these and is proceeding with
both types of schemes in relation to short as well as long-term goals.
The Tamilnadu Government has similarly recognized such needs and
is proceeding accordingly.[8] And this is to the credit of both governments, for the policy of many governments generally has been
either *laissez-faire* or marked only by rigid controls rather than
development schemes.
The efforts of these governments have been impressive and the
accomplishments real. Nevertheless, in general, slum peoples are
still treated as "disorganized," burdened by "slum mentalities" and
so on. And this we are assuming (see Chapter One) is too costly

and misguiding a perspective to adhere to, especially if it is factually incorrect.

Now again, the extent to which such descriptions can be suitably used cannot be determined in relation to our study. But our conclusions about the Chennanagar people — conclusions derived after looking at the conditions of life from "within" the context — have to encourage us to see these and similar people as able to help themselves in many ways.

By no means can this imply that such people should be left alone. The Chennanagar people need the guarantee of sufficient municipal services and public utility supplies, and they need the guarantee of access to the officials and authorities responsible for their welfare. They need health care and educational facilities. They need to be able to continue to tie themselves into the various networks that characterize their various environments even as they now do. And they need the benefits implicit in the kinds of development schemes the involved governments are conducting for their benefit.

The people in places like Chennanagar need help. But they also need to be recognized as able to function effectively, resourcefully, and in organized ways. They need to be recognized as able to understand their own needs and expectations. Despite their poverty, they can.

REFERENCES

[1] Oscar Lewis, *La Vida*, Vintage Books of Random House, New York, 1966, p. xliv.

[2] Oscar Lewis, "Peasant Culture in India and Mexico: A Comparative Analysis," in M. Marriot, *Village India*, *op. cit.*, pp. 145-170.

[3] The best material on this is W.H. Wiser and C. Wiser, *Behind Mud Walls*, University of California Press, Berkeley, 1963.

[4] I am indebted to Professor Gerald Suttles for reminding me again of some of these ideas after his reading of an earlier draft of this book, and for the phrase quoted.

[5] P. Ramachandran, "The Slum, A Note on Facts and Solutions," in A.R. Desai and S.D. Pillai, *Slums and Urbanization*, Popular Prakashan, Bombay, 1970, pp. 166-167.

[6] P. Ramachandran, *ibid.*, p. 168.

[7] D.R. Gadgil, "Housing and Slums of Poona," in *The Economic Weekly*, XI, 14 April 1959.

[8] Chapter Two gives some information about slum clearance and development schemes in Madras. Part IV — Section 4, Tamilnadu Acts and Ordinances, Government of Tamilnadu, 1971, gives the latest legal understandings.

Bibliography

ADAMS, J. and UWE J. WOLTEMADE, "Village Economy in Traditional India: A Simplified Model," in *Human Organization*, 29 (Spring), 1970.

ANNADURAI, C.N., "DMK as I See It," in Iqbal Narain (ed.), *State Politics in India*, Meenakshi Prakashan, Meerut, 1967.

BAILEY, F.G., *Politics and Social Change*, University of California Press, Berkeley, 1959.

———, "Structure and Change in Indian Society: A Review Article," in *Pacific Affairs*, XLII (Winter), 1969.

BALASUNDARAM, S.N., "The Dravidian (Non-Brahmin) Movement in Madras," in Iqbal Narain (ed.), *State Politics in India, op. cit.*

BETEILLE, ANDRE, *Caste, Class and Power*, University of California Press, Berkeley, 1965.

BHARATI, AGEHANANDA, "Hinduism and Modernization," in Robert Spencer (ed.), *Religion and Change in Contemporary Asia*, University of Minnesota Press, Minneapolis, 1971.

BOMBAY MUNICIPAL CORPORATION, "Slums of Bombay," in A.R. Desai and S.D. Pillai (eds.), *Slums and Urbanization*, Popular Prakashan, Bombay, 1970.

BOSE, "The Process of Urbanization in India: Some Emerging Issues," in Richard G. Fox (ed.), *Urban India: Society, Space and Image*, Duke University Press, 1970.

BOSWELL, JOHN A.C., *Manual of the Nellore District*, Government Press, Madras, 1873.

BOTTOMORE, T.B., "Modern Elites in India," in T.K.N. Unnithan, Indra Dev, and Yogendra Singh (eds.), *Towards a Sociology of Culture in India*, Prentice-Hall, New Delhi, 1965.

BROWN, W. NORMAN, "The Content of Cultural Continuity in India," in *Journal of Asian Studies*, XX, August 1961.

CARSTAIRS, G.M., *The Twice-Born: A Study of a Community of High Caste Hindus*, Indiana University Press, Bloomington, 1961.

CENSUS OF INDIA, 1961, Madras, vol. 9, Part 10 (III).

CHANDRASEKHAR, S., "Growth of Population in Madras City, 1639-1961," in *Population Review*, 8, January 1964.

CORPORATION OF MADRAS, "District Family Planning Bureau on the Pathway to Progress," mimeographed circular, 1970.

DALTON, DENNIS, "The Gandhian View of Caste and Caste after Gandhi," in Phillip Mason (ed.), *India and Ceylon: Unity and Diversity*, Oxford University Press, London, 1967.

DANDEKAR, V.M., and N. RATH, "Poverty in India," in *Economic and Political Weekly*, VI, 2 January 1971.

DAS, R.K., *Temples of Tamilnadu*, Bharatiya Vidya Bhavan, Bombay, 1964.

DATTATRI, G., and S.D. RAJ, "Urbanization in India: Planning for a Balanced Urban Planning and Structure," mimeographed paper presented at the seminar, "Urban Planning for a Greater India," Dasaprakash Hotel, Madras, 6 July 1967.

DESAI, A.R., and S.D. PILLAI, Slums and Urbanization, op. cit.

DESAI, P.B., "Economy of Indian Cities," in The Journal of Public Administration, XIV, July-September 1968.

DEVANANDAN, P.D., The Gospel and Renascent Hinduism, S.C.M. Press, London, 1959.

The Dravida Kazagham: A Revolt Against Brahminism, Christian Institute for the Study of Religion and Society, Bangalore, 1960.

DEWETT, K.K., D.C. SINGH, and J.D. VARMA, Indian Economics, S. Chand and Co. Ltd., Delhi, 1971.

DODWELL, H., "The History of Madras," in Indian Science Congress Handbook, Diocesan Press, Madras, 1921.

DUBE, S.C., Indian Village, Routledge and Kegan Paul, London, 1955.

EISENSTADT, S.N., "Some Remarks on Patterns of Change in Traditional and Modern India," in K. Ishwaran (ed.), Change and Continuity in India's Villages, Columbia University Press, New York, 1970.

ELMORE, W.T., Dravidian Gods in Modern Hinduism, Christian Literature Society Press, Madras, 1925.

EPSTEIN, T.S., Economic Development and Social Change in South India, Manchester University Press, Manchester, 1962.

FIRTH, C.B., An Introduction to Indian Church History, The Christian Literature Society, Madras, 1961.

GOVERNMENT OF INDIA, Publications Division, Temples in South India, Government Publications auspices, Delhi, 1960.

GOVERNMENT OF TAMILNADU, Finance Department, Tamilnadu: An Economic Appraisal, 1971-72, Government Publications auspices, Madras, 1971.

Tamilnadu Government Gazette Extraordinary, Government Publications auspices, Madras, 15 January 1971.

GADGIL, D.R., "Housing and Slums of Poona," in The Economic Weekly, XI, 14 April 1959.

GALANTER, M., "The Religious Aspects of Caste: A Legal View," in D. Smith (ed.), South Asian Politics and Religion, Princeton University Press, 1966.

GALBRAITH, J.K., The Affluent Society, Hamish Hamilton, London, 1958.

GANS, HERBERT J., The Urban Villagers, Free Press of Glencoe, New York, 1962.

GHURYE, G.S., Caste and Class in India, Popular Book Depot, Bombay, 1957.

GOULD, HAROLD A. "The Adaptive Functions of Caste in Contemporary Indian Society," in Asian Survey, III, September 1963.

"Time Dimension and Structural Change in an Indian Kinship System: A Problem of Conceptual Refinement," in Milton Singer and Bernard S. Cohn (eds.), Structure and Change in Indian Society, Aldine Publishing Company, Chicago, 1968.

"Toward a Jati-Model for Indian Political Relations," in Economic and Political Weekly, IV, 1 February 1969.

GUMPERZ, JOHN J., "Religion and Social Communication¯ in Village North India," in Edward B. Harper (ed.), *Religion in South Asia*, University of Washington Press, Seattle, 1964.

GUPTA, S.K., "Slums," p. 210 in the Government of India publication issued on behalf of the Planning Commission, *Encyclopedia of Social Work in India*, vol. 2, 1968.

GUSFIELD, J.R., "Political Community and Group Interests in Modern India," in *Pacific Affairs*, 38, 1965.

"Tradition and Modernity: Misplaced Polarities in the Study of Social Change," in *American Journal of Sociology*, 72, January 1967.

HARDGRAVE, ROBERT L., Jr., *The Dravidian Movement*, Popular Prakashan, Bombay, 1965.

"Religion, Politics and the DMK," in D. Smith (ed.), *South Asian Politics and Religion, op. cit.*

HIEBERT, PAUL G., *Konduru: Structure and Integration in a South Indian Village*, University of Minnesota Press, Minneapolis, 1971.

IMPERIAL GAZETTEER OF INDIA, *The Indian Empire* (vol. 2), *Historical*, The Clarendon Press, Oxford, 1908.

ISHWARAN, K. (ed.), *Change and Continuity in India's Villages, op. cit.*,

JHA, CHETKAR, *India's Self Government*, Patna, 1953.

KAPP, K. WILLIAM, *Hindu Culture, Economic Development and Economic Planning in India*, Asia Publishing House, Bombay, 1963.

KARVE, IRAVATI, *Kinship Organization in India*, Asia Publishing House, Bombay, 1965.

KOLENDA, PAULINE M., "Toward a Model of the Hindu Jajmani System," in *Human Organization*, XXII, 1963.

"Religion, Caste and Family Structure: A Comparative Study of the Indian Joint Family," in Milton Singer and Bernard S. Cohn (eds.), *Structure and Change in Indian Society, op. cit.*

"What Changes are Occurring in the Structure of the Indian Joint Family?" Paper presented at the Interdisciplinary Conference on Processes of Change in Contemporary Asian Societies, University of Illinois, Champaign-Urbana, 5-7 November 1970.

"Family Structure in Village Lonikand, India: 1819, 1958 and 1967," in *Contributions to Indian Sociology*, IV, December 1970.

KRISHNASWAMY, S.Y., *Kalyani's Husband*, Higginbotham's Private Limited, Madras, 1967.

KUMAR, RAVINDER, "Rural Life in Western India on the Eve of the British Conquest," in *The Indian Economic and Social History*, II, July 1965.

LANCHESTER, H.V., *Town Planning in Madras*, Constable and Company, Limited, London, 1918.

LAQUIAN, APRODICIO A., "Slums and Squatters in South and Southeast Asia," in Leo Jakobson and Ved Prakash (eds.), *Urbanization and National Development*, Sage Publications, Beverly Hills, 1971.

LEWIS, OSCAR, "Peasant Culture in India and Mexico: A Comparative Analysis," in M. Marriott (ed.), *Village India*, University of Chicago Press, Chicago, 1955.

La Vida, Vintage Books of Random House, New York, 1966.

"Reply to Valentine," in *Current Anthropology*, 10 April-June 1969.

LIEBOW ELLIOTT, *Tailey's Corner: A Study of Negro Streetcorner Men*, Little Brown and Company, Boston, 1967.

LYNCH, OWEN M., "Rural Cities in India: Continuities and Discontinuities," in Phillip Mason (ed.), *India and Ceylon: Unity and Diversity, op. cit.*

MADAN, G.R., *India's Social Problems: Social Disorganization*, Allied Publishers, Bombay, 1969.

MADRAS SCHOOL OF SOCIAL WORK, *Social Welfare in the Slums of Madras*, New India Publishers, Madras, 1965.

MARRIOTT, M., Little Communities in an Indigenous Civilization," in M. Marriott (ed.), *Village India, op. cit.*

"Interactional and Attributional Theories of Caste Ranking," in *Man in India*, 39, 1959.

"The Feast of Love," in M. Singer (ed.), *Krishna: Myths, Rites and Attitudes*, East-West Center Press, Honolulu, 1966.

"Multiple Reference in India's Caste System," in John Silverberg (ed.), *Social Mobility in the Caste System in India*, Mouton Publishers, London, 1968.

MARRIOTT, M. (ed.), *Village India, op. cit.*

MASON, PHILLIP, "Unity and Diversity: An Introductory Review," in Philip Mason (ed.), *India and Ceylon: Unity and Diversity, op. cit.*

MATZA, DAVID, "Reply to Valentine," in *Current Anthropology*, 10, April-June 1969.

MENCHER, JOAN P., "A Tamil Village: Changing Socio-Economic Structure in Madras State," in K. Ishwaran (ed.), *Change and Continuity in India's Villages, op. cit.*

MOLONY, J.C., *A Book of South India*, Methuen & Co. Ltd., London, 1926.

MUKERJEE, RAMAKRISHNA, *The Sociologist and Social Change in India Today*, Prentice-Hall, New Delhi, 1965.

NAMBIAR, P.K., *Slums of Madras City*, vol. 9 (Madras), Part X1-C, *Census of India*, 1961.

NARASIMHAM, K.L., *Madras City: A History*, Rachana, Madras, 1968.

NAYAK, P.R., "Community Development: Urban," p. 132 in the Government of India publication issued on behalf of the Planning Commission, *Encyclopaedia of Social Work in India*, vol. 1, 1968.

NEILL, STEPHEN, *The Cross over Asia*, The Canterbury Press, London, 1948. *Christian Faith and Other Faiths*, Oxford University Press, London, 1961.

PALMER, NORMAN D., *The Indian Political System*, Houghton Mifflin Company, Boston, 1961.

PARK, RICHARD L., *India's Political System*, Prentice-Hall, Inc., Englewood Cliffs, New Jersey, 1967.

PEATTIE, LISA R., *The View from the Barrio*, University of Michigan Press, Ann Arbor, 1968.

PETHE, V.P., *Demographic Profiles of an Urban Population*, Popular Prakashan, Bombay, 1964.

PENNY, Mrs. FRANK, *Fort St. George, Madras*, Swan Sonnenschien and Co. Ltd., London, 1900.

PRATT, J.B., *India and its Faiths*, Houghton Mifflin Company, Boston, 1915.

RADHAKRISHNAN, S., *East and West in Religion*, George Allen and Unwin, London, 1954.

Eastern Religions and Western Thought, Oxford University Press, New York, 1959.

RAGHAVAN, O.T., "Water and Sanitation," mimeographed paper presented at the seminar, "Urban Planning for a Greater India," Dasaprakash Hotel, Madras, 6 July 1967.

RAMACHANDRAN, P., "The Slum: A Note on Facts and Solutions," in A.R. Desai and S.D. Pillai (eds.), *Slums and Urbanization, op. cit.*

RAMANA, K.V., "Caste and Society in an Andhra Town," unpublished Ph.D. dissertation, University of Illinois, Champaign-Urbana, 1970.

RAMU, G.N., "Factors that Retard Family Planning Movement," in *Family Planning News*, June 1968.

"Family and Kinship in Urban South India," unpublished Ph.D. dissertation, University of Illinois, Champaign-Urbana, 1972.

RAMU, G.N., and PAUL D. WIEBE, "Profiles of Rural Politics in Mysore," in *Eastern Anthropologist*, XXIII, May-August 1970.

RANSON, C.W., *A City in Transition: Studies in the Social Life of Madras*, The Christian Literature Society, Madras, 1938.

REDFIELD, ROBERT, *The Little Community: Viewpoints for the Study of a Human Whole*, University of Chicago Press, Chicago, 1955.

RICE, B. LEWIS, *Mysore: A Gazetteer Compiled for Government*, Archibald Constable and Company, Westminister, 1897.

RUDOLF, LLOYD I., and SUSANNE H., *The Modernity of Tradition: Political Development in India*, University of Chicago Press, Chicago, 1967.

SEN, S.N., "Exerpts from The City of Calcutta: A Socio-Economic Survey (1954-55 to 1957-58)," in A.R. Desai and S.D. Pillai (eds.), *Slums and Urbanization, op. cit.*

SERVICE CIVIL INTERNATIONAL AND THE SWALLOWS (Urban Rehabilitation Project), "Social-Economic Survey: Family Case Study," n.d.

SHIVARAMAN, MYTHILY, "The Dravida Munnetra Kazagham: The Content of its Ideology," in *The Radical Review*, I, Madras, 1970.

SINGER, MILTON, "The Great Tradition in a Metropolitan Center," in *Journal of American Folklore*, 71 July-September 1958.

"The Radhakrishna Bhajans of Madras City," in *History of Religion*, 2, (Winter) 1963.

"The Social Organization of Indian Civilization," in *Diogenes*, 45, April 1964.

"The Indian Joint Family in Modern Industry," in Milton Singer and Bernard S. Cohn (eds.), *Structure and Change in Indian Society, op. cit.*

When a Great Tradition Modernizes: An Anthropological Approach to Indian Civilization, Praeger Publishers, New York, 1972.

SMITH, W.C., "The Ulama in Indian Politics," in C.H. Philips (ed.), *Politics and Society in India*, George Allen and Unwin, Ltd., London, 1963.

SOVANI, N.V., *Urbanization and Urban India*, Asia Publishing House, Bombay, 1966.

SOVANI, N.V., *et. al.*, *Poona: A Resurvey: The Changing Patterns of Employment and Earnings*, Gokhale Institute of Politics and Economics, Poona, 1956.

SPRATT, P., *DMK in Power*, Nachiketa, Bombay, 1970.

SRINIVAS, M.N., *Religion and Society Among the Coorgs of South India*, Oxford University Press, London, 1952.
Caste in Modern India and Other Essays, Asia Publishing House, Madras, 1962.
Social Change in Modern India, University of California Press, Berkeley, 1966.
SRINIVAS, M.N. (ed.), *India's Villages*, Asia Publishing House, New York, 1960.
STOKES, CHARLES J., "A Theory of Slums," in *Land Economics*, XXXXVIII, April 1962.
SUTTLES, GERALD, *The Social Order of the Slum*, University of Chicago Press, Chicago, 1968.
TAMILNADU DIRECTORATE OF TOWN PLANNING, *Interim Plan: Madras Metropolitan Area, 1970-71*, mimeographed.
THILLAINAYAGAM, R., "Transportation Planning," mimeographed paper presented at the seminar, "Urban Planning for a Greater India," Dasaprakash Hotel, Madras, 6 July 1967.
THURSTON, EDGAR, *Castes and Tribes of Southern India* (7 volumes), Government Press, Madras, 1909.
TINKER, HUGH, "Is there an Indian Nation?" in Phillip Mason (ed.), *India and Ceylon: Unity and Diversity, op. cit.*
TOWNSEND, PETER, "The Meaning of Poverty," in *British Journal of Sociology*, 13 (September) 1962.
TRIVEDI, R.K., "Special Report on Ahmedabad City," vol. V (Gujarat), Part XA-i, *Census of India*, 1961.
UNITED NATIONS, "Urbanization: Development Policies and Planning," in *International Social Development Review*, no. 1, 1968.
VALENTINE, CHARLES A., *Culture and Poverty*, University of Chicago Press, Chicago, 1968.
"Culture and Poverty: Critique and Counter-Proposals," in *Current Anthropology*, 10, April-June 1969.
WARREN, R.L., *The Community in America*, Rand McNally and Company, Chicago, 1963.
WAX, ROSALIE, *Doing Fieldwork: Warnings and Advice*, University of Chicago Press, Chicago, 1971.
WEBER, MAX, *The Religion of India*, The Free Press, Glencoe, 1958.
WEINSTEIN, JAY, "The Factorial Ecology of Madras," unpublished Ph.D. dissertation, University of Illinois, Champaign-Urbana, 1972.
WHEELER, J. TALBOYS, *Madras in the Olden Times*, 1639-1748, Calcutta, 1878.
WHITEHEAD, H., *Gods and Goddesses of South India*, Oxford University Press, 1921.
WIEBE, PAUL D., "Small Town in Modern India," unpublished Ph.D. dissertation, University of Kansas, Lawrence, 1969.
"Elections in Peddur: Democracy at Work in an Indian Town," in *Human Organization*, 28, Summer, 1969.
"Christianity and Social Change in South India," in *Practical Anthropology*, 17, May-June 1970.

"Protestant Missions in India: A Sociological Review," in *Journal of Asian and African Studies*, 5, October 1970.

WIEBE, PAUL D., and G.N. RAMU, "Marriage in India: A Content Analysis of Matrimonial Advertisements," in *Man in India*, 51, April-June 1971.

WISER, W.H., "The Economics of Poverty," in *The Allahabad Farmer*, X, November 1936.

WISER, W.H. and C., *Behind Mud Walls*, University of California Press, Berkeley, 1963.

ZINKIN, TAYA, *Caste Today*, Oxford University Press, London, 1962.

Index

Adi-Dravidas, migration pattern of, 23-24
ADMK, role of, 107
Annadurai, C.N., role of, 105; stature of, 108

Bombay State, 1960, reorganization of, 104
Bose, Ashish, on party politics in community service, 38

Caste, and Hinduism, 56, 126-127; and kin, interrelation between, 59; and politics, 69-70; definition of, 59
Caste groups, enumeration of, 60
Chandrasekhar, S., population studies by, 19, 20
Chennanagar, and culture of poverty, 160-161; and Indian social attitudes and organization, 162-163; attitudes to work in, 94-95; caste feelings in, 68-69; caste identification analysis, 61-72, 155; caste statistics of, 62, civic amenities for, 46-47; community characteristics of, 77-78, 156-157; compared with other world slum communities, 164; death ceremonies in, 133-134; debt pattern in, 99-100; distribution of family types in, 75-76; education in, 162-163; election politics in, 109-113; employment pattern, in, 92-94; environmental interrelationship of, 157-159; expenditure distribution by major items (1971), 96; family life in, 159; family planning in, 149-151;

family ties in, 155; household worship in, 131; inter-class marriages in, 67; life in, 153-154; life cycle ceremonies in, 132-134; living conditions in, 41-44; *Manram* politics in, 113-117, 155-156; marriage ceremonies in, 133; marriage expenditures in, 96-97; methodology for study of, 12-13; occupational identifications in, 87-91; population by first language, 50; population by sex, age, and literacy, 49-50; population distribution by per capita income (1970), 86-87; public worship in, 128-131; reasons for study of, 11-12; recreation and social life in, 48; religious influences in, 138-139; savings and investment pattern in, 97-99; settlement of, 39-41; schooling facilities in, 144-146; social life in, 154-155; water supply problem of, 44-46
Chit Funds, popularity of, 99
Community, definition of, 77
Congress Party, 39, 45, 52
Congress vs. DMK, 106, 109
Constitution of India, federal features of, 104-105
Culture of poverty, analysis of, 9-10; features of, 154

Democracy, features of, 103-104
DK, role of, 105
DMK, 33, 39, 45; anti-Brahmin teachings of, 127, 137; rise of, 106-107; role of, 105; social role of, 64

Dravidian movement, anti-Brahmanism of, 64; features of, 105-106
Dupleix, role of, 17

East India Company, establishment
in South India, 17
Education and employment, 143
Elections, role of caste and money
in, 111-112

Family Planning, in Five Year Plans,
146
Fort St. George, history of, 17

Gandhi, Mahatma, impact on Indian
people, 70

Hinduism, and caste, 126-127;
resurgence of, 127, 135
Hyder Ali, role of, 77

India, linguistic reorganization of
states (1956), 104; North vs. South,
104-105; Tamilnadu and Madras
populations, distribution by religion, 124
Indian population, distribution by per
capita consumer expenditure (1960-
61), 83-84
Indian social organization, features of,
58-61; modernization of, 61; traditional patterns of, 8
Indian village, social features of, 160
Indian village studies, Chicago
University seminar on, 60
Industrial society, impact on family
structure, 76

Jajmani system, 91-92
Jati model (of Indian politics), 120
Joint/extended/nuclear families, des-
cription of, 59

Justice Party (South Indian Liberal
Federation), role of, 105

Kamraj, role of, 69
Kipling, Rudyard, on Madras, 24

Life cycle ceremonies, practice of.
131-134

Madras; administrative organization
of, 108; climate and geography of,
26; composition structure of, 6;
employment pattern in, 23; Family
Planning progress in, 146-147;
founding and initial development of,
17-18; Islam and Christianity in,
128; manifestation of Hinduism in,
125; population by first language,
50-51; population by sex, age, and
literacy, 49; population growth
(1639-1961), 18-21; present development of, 22-23; present day life in,
25-26; see also Slums in Madras;
water supply, problem of, 29
Manrams, 109-121
Marriages, 96-97; caste considerations
in, 66-67

Nawab of Carnatic, British influence
over, 18
Nehru, Jawaharlal, impact on
Indian people, 70

Panchayati Raj, features of, 103
Party politics in community services,
example of, 52
Patronage, and money, role of, 118-
120
Politics of scarcity, example of, 45
Poverty, definition of, 7-8
Poverty in India, and gains of develop-
ment, 84; dimensions of, 1-2

Ramachandran, M.G., role of, 107, 110

Ramaswamy, Naicker, 127; role of, 105

Ranking system, metropolitan vs. rural, 71-72

Ranson, C.W., on Adi-Dravidas, 23-24

Refugees (from Burma and Ceylon), and growth of Madras slums, 31

Religion, hold in rural India, 126

Religious beliefs and practices, changes in, 135; and cultural traditions, 135-137

Rural India, social organization of, 58

Sanskritization, process of, 60, 67

Slums, and surrounding environments, 5-6; definition of, 27-28

Slum clearance and improvement, approach to, 7; in Madras, 33, 163; policies relating to, 164-166

Slums in India, available studies on, 2-4; problem of, 2

Slums in Madras, 1961 census study on, 27; clearance and improvement of, 33; family planning in, 147-149; features and problems of, 28-30; kinds of, 30-31; number and population of, 28; reasons for growth of, 31-32; social service in, 32, 47

Special Housing Committee, 1933 (Madras Corporation), estimates on Madras slums, 28

Spiritual and magical practices, popularity of, 137-138

Tamil, cultural heritage of, 6

Tamilnadu, educational problems of, 142-143; family planning progress in, 146-147; population by first language, 50-51; population distribution by per capita consumer expenditure in, 85; "Tamilization" of politics in, 69

Tamilnadu Slum Clearance Board, 25, 33

Telengana-Andhra District, 104

Tippu Sultan, role of, 17

Treaty of Aix-la-Chapelle (1749), 17

Untouchability, enactment against, 70

Varna, classificatory features of, 59